WHO

DO YOU THINK YOU ARE?

WHO

DO YOU THINK YOU ARE?

THE ESSENTIAL GUIDE TO TRACING YOUR FAMILY HISTORY

DAN WADDELL

This book is published to accompany the television series
Who Do You Think You Are? produced by Wall to Wall Media Ltd.

Series Editor: Ben Gale
Series Producer: Victoria Watson
Executive Producers: Alex Graham, Alex West

Published by BBC Books, BBC Worldwide Ltd
Woodlands
80 Wood Lane
London W12 0TT

ISBN: 0 563 52194 5

Commissioning Editor: Sally Potter
Project Editor: Sarah Emsley
Copy Editor: Tessa Clark
Art Director: Linda Blakemore
Design: DW Design, London
Picture Researcher: Charlotte Lochhead
Production Controller: Christopher Tinker

Origination by Butler & Tanner Ltd
Printed and bound in Great Britain by CPI Bath

INTRODUCTION

LAST YEAR I BECAME A FATHER
FOR THE FIRST TIME. I WAS NOT
TOO BOTHERED ABOUT THE SEX
OF MY CHILD BEFORE THE BIRTH,
BUT WHEN WE DISCOVERED IT
WAS A BOY I REALIZED THIS
GUARANTEED THAT THE FAMILY
NAME, WADDELL, WOULD
CONTINUE FOR AT LEAST
ANOTHER GENERATION. TO MY
SURPRISE I FOUND SATISFACTION
IN THIS, PRIDE EVEN.

THEN I WONDERED WHY; IT WAS JUST A NAME, AFTER ALL, AND BEFORE MY SON'S BIRTH MY INTEREST IN FAMILY HISTORY HAD BEEN NEGLIGIBLE, TO PUT IT MILDLY. I STARTED TO THINK OF MY FAMILY'S PAST, AND THE PATH THAT HAD LED TO THE PRESENT. WHO WERE THE HEROES AND VILLAINS? I SPOKE TO MY FATHER ABOUT WHAT HE KNEW OF OUR HISTORY. IT TURNED OUT HE HAD ALREADY MADE SOME TENTATIVE INQUIRIES; A WADDELL HAD BEEN A UNION NAVAL CAPTAIN IN THE AMERICAN CIVIL WAR, BLOWING UP BRITISH SHIPS FERRYING COTTON FROM THE SOUTH; ANOTHER HAD BEEN PART OF A GROUP WHO HAD FOUNDED THE PONY EXPRESS. COULD ONE OF THESE BE AN ANCESTOR OF OURS? I BEGAN A SEARCH AND QUICKLY ESTABLISHED THAT THE YANKEE SEAFARING CAPTAIN WAS NOT A CLOSE RELATIVE. YET WITHIN A FEW HOURS I DID UNCOVER A FAMILY SECRET THAT HAD LAIN UNDISTURBED FOR MORE THAN HALF A CENTURY. AS A REFORMED TABLOID JOURNALIST – WELL, ALMOST REFORMED – THIS WHIFF OF SCANDAL AWOKE MY CURIOSITY; MY APPETITE WAS WHETTED.

I tell you this not to bore you with my family history, but to illustrate, as the BBC series that accompanies this book also does, that genealogy is not simply an endless trawl through fusty files; it is a quest that can lead to the most astonishing revelations. The best thing about it is that you do not know in which direction this quest will take you. You may discover that your Great-great-uncle Alfred was involved in the Charge of the Light Brigade; or that Great-aunt Gertie was at the forefront of the suffragette movement. Perhaps not. It may turn out you are descended from honest working folk with no spectacular secrets or heroic deeds to reveal. But what you will discover is that your ancestors were human beings who lived and loved. They were not simply part of history: they are history. Our ancestors may not have been famous or made appearances in the history books, but they are the stuff of real history. Along the way you will find answers about who you are and what informs your passions, prejudices and convictions, as well as encountering some of the major events that shaped modern Britain.

Family historians are like detectives, piecing together clues, dispelling myths, not taking things at face value, building a picture of how and why their ancestors lived as they did. This is a journey that you can take as far as you wish, depending on your goals and your appetite for the chase. It may be that, like me, you simply want to track down the heroes and villains in your family's past; you may live abroad, in places such as Australia or the USA, and want to track your English ancestors; or perhaps you want to trace your lineage back to William the Conqueror (though beware, it is practically impossible to do so); you might even want to produce an elaborately drawn family tree to give to your relatives, as a legacy perhaps. The choice is yours entirely. Family history is not a

> **Genealogy is not simply an endless trawl through fusty files; it is a quest that can lead to the most astonishing revelations.**

Producing an elaborate family tree will save future genealogists in your family a lot of hard work.

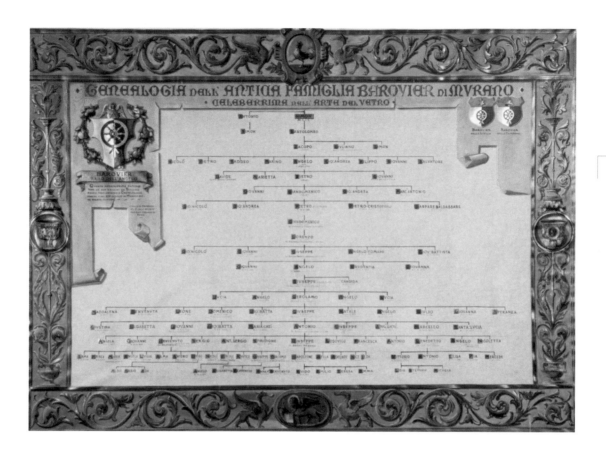

< **Genealogy is the third most popular pursuit on the Internet (behind personal finance and, er, porn).** >

full-time pursuit; you can dip in and out whenever it suits you. Your ancestors are not going anywhere. How you approach your search is entirely in your hands.

Be warned, however: it is easy to become wrapped up in searching for elusive forebears. Once you take the plunge, the search can gather its own unstoppable momentum. You may find yourself thinking of little else, baffling your friends and family by speaking of an 'exciting' death certificate you are waiting for, or by preparing a packed lunch of potted-meat sandwiches and a vacuum flask of weak lemon squash for an all-day stint at the Family Records Centre.

The purpose of this book is to equip you with the basic tools you need to start and maintain your quest. The assumption is that you have no knowledge at all of family history; that you are an absolute beginner. It is easy to become intimidated by the mass of material that exists, or the prospect of entering a record office and having to interpret the data you find there. Hopefully, this book will allay any doubts and show how easy and accessible family history is. The initial chapters deal with the basics: tasks that anyone, whether or not they are serious about tracing their ancestors, should tick off. The later chapters describe some of the routes your search may go down and furnish you with the skills you need to add meat to bones and discover more than simply when and where your ancestors were born, married and died, but also how they lived, the events that shaped their lives and the social conditions in which they existed. Along the way there are tips for getting the most out of your research and, where relevant, recommendations for using the Internet so that you can further your search from the comfort of your own home.

Happy hunting.

opposite: Medieval depiction of imperial genealogy from Liber Chronicarum, *created by Michael Wohlgemuth, c. July 1493.*

GETTING STARTED

TO TRACE THE **DEAD**, IT IS BEST TO START WITH THE LIVING. **THIS BOOK** BEGINS WITH THE PREMISE THAT YOU HAVE LITTLE OR NO KNOWLEDGE OF YOUR FAMILY HISTORY. **THEREFORE**, THE COMMON-SENSE PLACE TO EMBARK ON YOUR SEARCH IS WITH PEOPLE WHO DO. **THINK** OF ALL THE MEMBERS OF YOUR FAMILY WHO ARE STILL ALIVE AND WOULD BE WILLING TO TALK TO YOU. **BEAR IN MIND** THAT FOR SOME PEOPLE THE PAST IS A CLOSED BOOK AND THEY WOULD PREFER IT TO REMAIN THAT WAY. **THERE IS NO POINT** IN ATTEMPTING TO CAJOLE SOMEONE INTO SPEAKING WITH YOU AGAINST THEIR WILL; 'DOORSTEPPING' YOUR UNCLE FRED LIKE A TABLOID JOURNALIST AND TRYING TO PERSUADE HIM TO TALK WON'T WORK. **INSTEAD**, IT IS BEST TO UNDERSTAND AND RESPECT **PEOPLE'S PRIVACY**.

IF YOU HAVE RELATIVES who are willing to speak to you then your quest can begin. (For those of you without any living older relatives, fear not; see 'Putting Yourself First' on page 66.) Before visiting anyone or speaking to them on the phone, it is a good idea to draw a rough family tree of what you already know. At this stage it might consist only of yourself and your parents, and perhaps your grandparents if you are lucky. Keeping a family tree – details on how to do this are given later – helps you to see where the gaps that need to be filled are, and these can provide a focus for your questions and future research.

Let's assume that you have a found an elderly relative who is happy to speak to you about your family's past. If you are going to interview them in person, make sure you are prepared. Write down beforehand the questions you want answers to; take either a notebook to record answers and information or, better still, take a tape recorder, which will free you from having to scribble notes continuously and allow you to listen more carefully. Be sure to inform your interviewee that you are recording the conversation. Once the interview has started, be patient; memories are often hazy and elusive, and time is needed to recapture them. A Jeremy

Did you know?

< **In the 1881 census, there is a GP listed with the surname De'ath. It doesn't record how many patients Dr De'ath had.** >

below: It helps to sketch out your family tree on a piece of paper as you go so you can see where the gaps are and where to target your search.

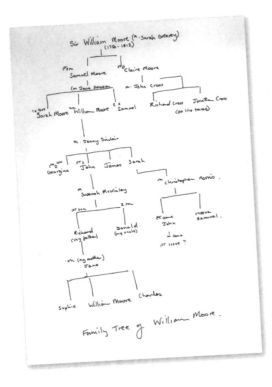

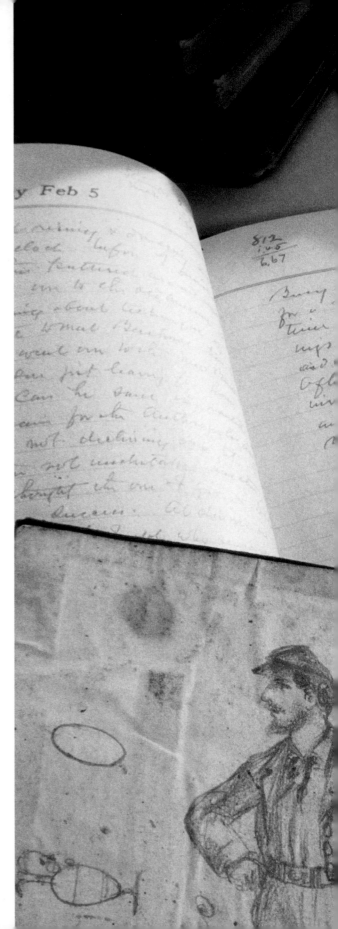

Paxman-style examination is not the best way to gain information from someone who is struggling to remember the past, or, for whatever reason, is unwilling to talk about it. All families have their secrets, scandals and black sheep, and there may be events in, or aspects of, a family history that people are unwilling to go over. Respect their feelings.

Any records your family members may possess and are willing to share with you are of great use. At the top of your 'wish list' should be birth, marriage and death certificates. These are manna from heaven for all family historians because of the invaluable information each

Old family documents, such as passports, not only aid your search, but can also be fascinating in their own right.

INTERVIEW **TIPS**

1 **Prepare. Think of the questions you might ask beforehand and write them down.**

2 **Take a notebook or tape recorder to record facts.**

3 **Be patient. Don't force people to answer questions if they don't want to.**

4 **Ask to see any letters, diaries, certificates or heirlooms your subject may possess.**

5 **Don't accept everything you are told as fact.**

medals and press cuttings. Be wary: these artefacts – old family photographs, for example – may need careful looking after, away from direct light, heat and damp. A good idea is to find an old shoebox to keep them in. If any heirlooms are damaged, or require restoration, seek professional help rather than getting creative with glue and sticky tape.

contains. They can act as a launch pad for your research. Seize upon any diaries and letters. Not only will these furnish you with information that will aid your search immediately; they may well also come in useful in the future, offering poignant insights when you are trying to understand why and how your ancestors lived as they did. Family photographs are helpful too (see 'Every Picture Tells a Story' on page 26), even though at first glance they may not seem to contain any useful information. Take ones showing unidentified people along with you to interviews to see whether your interviewee can identify them. Other heirlooms include war

If any heirlooms are damaged, or require restoration, seek professional help.

Certificate of Birth.

Pursuant to the Acts Anno Sexto et Septimo Gulielmi IV. Regis, Cap. LXXXVI, et Anno Primo Victoria Regina, Cap. XXII.

(Page 97)

1887   BIRTH in the District of Donhead in the County of Wilts

No.	When & Where Born	Name (if any)	Sex	Name and Surname of Father	Name and Maiden Surname of Mother	Rank or Profession of Father	Signature, Description, and Residence of Informant	When Registered	Signature of Registrar	Baptismal Name, if added after Registration of Birth
484	Fourth February 1887 Semley R.S.O.	Bertha Florence	Girl	Joseph Daniells	Mary Sarah Daniells formerly Baker	Railway Porter	Joseph Daniells Father Semley	Twenty Ninth March 1887	G. H. Ingram Registrar	

I, Registrar of Births and Deaths for the District of Donhead in the County of Wilts do hereby Certify the above to be a TRUE COPY of the BIRTH REGISTER, Entry No. 484 And I further Certify that the said REGISTER BOOK is legally in my custody.

Witness my hand this Twenty eighth day of March 1887   G. H. Ingram Registrar.

By the Statute 6 & 7 Will. IV, c. 86, s. 35, it is enacted "That every REGISTRAR, REGISTERING OFFICER, and SECRETARY, who shall have the keeping for the time being of any REGISTER BOOK of BIRTHS, DEATHS, or MARRIAGES, shall at all reasonable Times allow Searches to be made of any Register Book in his keeping, and shall give a COPY certified under his Hand of any ENTRY or Entries in the same, on payment of the Fee hereinafter mentioned; (that is to say) for every search extending over a period of not more than One Year the sum of One Shilling, and Sixpence additional for every additional Year, and the sum of Two Shillings and Sixpence for every single CERTIFICATE." (Including the Stamp the "Certificate" is Two Shillings and Sevenpence.)

B 19017

CERTIFIED COPY of an ENTRY OF BIRTH.
Pursuant to the Births and Deaths Registration Acts, 1836 to 1874.

[Printed by Authority of the Registrar General.]   B. Cert. R.B.D.

Registration District   Sevenoaks

1928   Birth in the Sub-District of Sevenoaks in the County of Kent

Columns:—	1	2	3	4	5	6	7	8	9	10
No.	When and Where Born	Name, if any.	Sex.	Name and Surname of Father	Name and Maiden Surname of Mother	Rank or Profession of Father	Signature, Description and Residence of Informant.	When Registered	Signature of Registrar.	Baptismal Name, if added after Registration of Birth.
328	Sixth April 1928 10 Chatham Hill Road Sevenoaks UD	Joanna Mary	Girl	Harry Lawson	Flora Bertha Lawson formerly Doxette	Railway Ticket Collector	H Lawson Father 10 Chatham Hill Road Sevenoaks	Ninth May 1928	A. Pratt Registrar.	

I, Arthur S. Pratt Registrar of Births and Deaths for the Sub-District of Sevenoaks in the County of Kent do hereby certify that this is a true copy of the Entry No. 325 in the Register Book of Births for the said Sub-district, and that such Register Book is now legally in my custody. WITNESS MY HAND this 9th day of May, 1928.

S. Pratt
Registrar of Births and Deaths.

DI 367107

B. Cert.
R.B.D.

[Printed by Authority of the Registrar General.]

The Statutory Fee for this Certificate is 3s. 9d. Where a search is necessary to find the entry, a Search Fee is payable in addition.

CERTIFIED COPY of an ENTRY OF BIRTH.
Pursuant to the Births and Deaths Registration Acts, 1836 to 1947.

Registration District   SURREY MID-EASTERN

1959   Birth in the Sub-District of   LEATHERHEAD   in the   COUNTY OF SURREY.

No.	When and where born.	Name, if any.	Sex.	Name and surname of father.	Name and maiden surname of mother.	Rank or profession of father.	Signature, description and residence of informant.	When registered.	Signature of Registrar.	Baptismal name, if added after registration of birth.
79	Thirty first July 1959, 491 Dorking Road Epsom, Epsom and Ewell U.D.	Steven Frank	Boy	Alan Ardouin Bill	Joanne May Bill formerly Lawson	Clerk (Borough Treasurers Department) of 39 Warren Road Banstead U.D.	Joanna M Bill Mother 39 Warren Road Banstead	Fifth August 1959	F.R. Mose Registrar.	

I,   , Registrar of Births and Deaths for the Sub-District of LEATHERHEAD , in the COUNTY OF SURREY, do hereby certify that this is a true copy of the Entry No. 75 in the Register Book of Births for the said Sub-District and that such Register Book is now legally in my custody.

WITNESS MY HAND this 5th day of August , 1959.

Registrar of Births and Deaths.

CAUTION.—Any person who (1) falsifies any of the particulars on this Certificate, or (2) uses it as true, knowing it to be falsified, is liable to Prosecution.

Birth certificates can be a treasure trove of information for genealogists. As these examples show, the style and content of birth certificates have changed over the last century. Here we have the certificates of four consecutive generations of a British family who were born in 1887, 1928, 1959, and 1989 respectively.

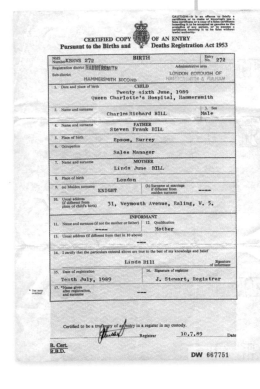

BILL ODDIE

THE ROOTS OF BILL ODDIE, or William Edgar Oddie to award him his full name as recorded on his birth certificate of 1941, shed a light on an intriguing era in working-class history. For Bill's ancestors worked and weaved in the 'dark Satanic mills' of Rochdale near Manchester, toiling in harsh conditions as distant to us now as the moon. Oddie's family history is one touched by tragedy and psychiatric illness. Indeed, he himself has twice suffered bouts of depression, a motivating factor in his quest to discover his roots. The story of his family encompasses several common themes; in particular, migration from the country to the city at the beginning of the Industrial Revolution.

Oddie grew up in Birmingham, in his own words 'a man with no family'. He is the only surviving child of a mentally ill mother, who he believed to be schizophrenic; a doting father, Harry; and a domineering grandmother, Emily, his main carer. His mother Lilian's illness cast a shadow over the family, as did the deaths of Oddie's two elder siblings, one was stillborn and the other, an older sister, choked to death within days of her birth. Whether these tragedies were a factor in triggering his mother's illness is a subject of debate, though surviving members of Oddie's family, such as his Aunt Margery, cast doubt on the diagnosis of schizophrenia. She remembers at least one doctor saying Lilian should never have been committed to a mental institution in the first place.

THE HUNT TO FIND the truth about his mother's illness – was she really schizophrenic or manic-depressive? – was inconclusive as her medical notes were destroyed. Bill remembers visiting her in hospital as a young boy and her not remembering him at all. This visit was perhaps a test of her sanity, and her failure to recognize him might have led to her being institutionalized for ten years. That loss of memory may not have been caused by her illness, however, but by the treatment for her condition. It was commonplace for those with mental illness to be treated by ECT – electroconvulsive therapy – a side effect of which is memory loss. Could this have been the reason she failed to remember her only son? Unfortunately for Bill, the truth will always remain a mystery.

Given these tragedies and his mother's illlness, the defining character of Bill's childhood was his grandmother. He has little positive to say about her – although he acknowledges that in his desire

Bill and his mother, Lilian, before she was committed to a mental institution.

to be out of the house and away from her, he developed his love of nature and specifically birds – and blames her for preventing him becoming close to his father, who was cowed and dominated by her. Research into her past, however, illustrates what an unforgiving life Emily Oddie had endured.

Emily's husband was Wilkinson Oddie, a cotton-weaver in the mills of Rochdale. According to the 1901 census, Wilkinson was a widower at the age of 36 and his eldest daughter, Betsy, was already working as a weaver at the tender age of 12. This was a family that knew hardship, and for a prolonged period. Wilkinson was to die on the operating table in 1927, a time when surgeons used chloroform as an anaesthetic for fear that the more gentle option, ether, would cause the operating theatre to be blown up. The irony was that Wilkinson suffered from a weak heart and chloroform is highly risky in such circumstances. Sadly, the risk proved too great and his heart gave out during the operation. An inquest into his death recorded that he had been suffering from throat cancer, a consequence of working conditions in the textile industry. Emily received no compensation for her husband's death.

Emily had met Wilkinson at the mill where they both worked and, at the age of 30, she took on his four children from his previous marriage – his first wife Cecilia had died at 31 giving birth to the couple's fifth child, who had also died. Emily would have had to struggle to raise the family after Wilkinson's demise – two years later the Great Depression ushered in an era of crushing poverty and punishing unemployment. Given all these circumstances, it is perhaps no surprise that Emily emerged as the hard and domineering woman Bill remembers. Yet such was her behaviour that he still cannot bring himself to forgive the grandmother who dominated the early years of his life so completely.

The story of Oddie's mother's family is also one of struggling to forge a living in the industrial north of England. His great-grandfather, Henry Bruckshaw, was a foreman in a Manchester match-making factory – the kind of place Karl Marx described in *Das Kapital* as being where 'only the most miserable part of the labouring class, half-starved widows and so forth, deliver their children'. These children worked in appalling, Dickensian conditions; by the age of 15 many of them were bald because of the heavy boxes they were required to carry on their heads. Cancer of the jawbone, 'phossy jaw' as it became known, was a common illness. Henry was a foreman, a management representative, and superior to the pitiful souls on the shop floor. However, research revealed that several of his relatives were workers in the same factory, which must have made for interesting conversations whenever – if ever – the family gathered together.

Henry was to meet a grisly end. While working as a semi-retired nightwatchman in his late sixties – a comfortable retirement was a luxury not extended to the working class back then – he tripped into a vat of boiling brine and died.

The Oddie family history was ultimately traced back to the early decades of the Industrial Revolution. Bill's great-grandfather on his father's side, John Oddie, worked in the mills during the cotton famine of 1861–5, when Union forces restricted the export of cotton from America's Deep South during the Civil War. His life was touched by tragedy: his first wife, Sarah Anne, died within two years of their marriage.

It was his father, and Bill's great-great-grandfather, another Wilkinson Oddie, who made the most pivotal move in the Oddies' early history. He moved his family from the village of Grindleton to

Bill and his father, Harry.

the mills of Blackburn in about the mid-1830s, presumably because the burgeoning industrialization of the textile industry made their cottage industry redundant. The 1820s and 1830s were a time of great unrest, as machines forced many home-based spinners and weavers out of business. It was in this climate, and in and around the areas where the Oddies lived, that social unrest fomented. Behind this were the Luddites, a group of disenchanted textile-workers who protested against the creeping rise in the use of machinery that was slowly crushing their industry. They attacked mills and broke machines, despite this being a criminal offence that carried the death penalty.

Research from parish registers revealed that the Oddies had been tenant labourers in Guisburn, close to Grindleton, until 1817, when a John Oddie (b. 1785) established the family business, spinning and weaving cloth in their cottage.

The history of Bill's family is a sober, often grim, parade of the travails and sufferings that befell Britain's working class during the Industrial Revolution. Yet it is also a story of triumph, of hardship overcome and tragedy conquered. Bill's father, Harry, was the first to be properly educated and consequently landed a white-collar job as an accountant – which raised the family from working-class penury. This then afforded Bill the opportunity to gain the qualifications that enabled him to go to Cambridge University and achieve his success. From the village of Guisburn to Bill's home in Hampstead, London, the story of the Oddie family is emblematic of Britain's transition from an age of cottage industries through the Industrial Revolution to the present, meritocratic age.

> **The story of Oddie's mother's family is also one of struggling to forge a living in the industrial north of England.**

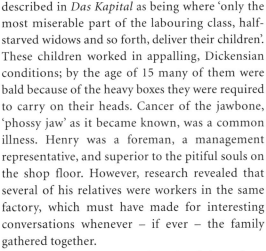

EVERY PICTURE
TELLS A STORY

SIMPLY STARING AT AN OLD FAMILY PHOTOGRAPH IS AN AMAZING EXPERIENCE. CAN WE SEE OURSELVES IN THE ANCESTORS PICTURED? BUT WHAT ELSE CAN THEY TELL US, OTHER THAN THE FACT THAT A BIG NOSE OR BALDNESS RUNS IN THE FAMILY?

1 Check the back of the photograph. Information on when and where it was taken, and who is in it, will often be written there.

2 What are people wearing? Dress, particularly women's, often suggests a date, or at least an era. For example, in the 1880s clothing was quite simple and plain, while in the 1860s and 1870s ribbons, frills and bows were the fashion.

3 If any of the men in the photograph are in military uniform, regimental buttons and caps may indicate the unit they served with.

left: Family portraits such as this can yield a great deal of information for family historians.

right: Dress and decor can help us to estimate the era in which photographs were taken.

A note of caution about interviews and the information you may obtain: don't accept what people tell you as fact. Myths and legends can easily become cemented as reality in the history of even the most sober family. Be wary when someone tells you that Great-grandfather was awarded a posthumous medal for bravery in the First World War. It may turn out he came home on leave, went to the pub and was knocked down by a bus as he staggered out – and to cover up that unflattering fact an alternative, rather more glamorous, myth was spread about his demise. Treat with scepticism claims that your family is descended from William the Conqueror, Henry VIII or King Canute. They may turn out to be true, but it is best to wait and find out for yourself.

Once you have completed your interviews, you may have a wealth of information, or you may have very little. Whichever, you need to record it in some way in order to ensure that

Treat with scepticism claims that your family is descended from William the Conqueror.

*Wedding photos are invaluable because every
member of the immediate family will often
feature in the picture.*

the next stage of your quest is successful. From now on you will be finding out more and more about your family's history and you need some way to arrange what you know to make it easy to access and interpret. Without some method of recording the information you uncover, it can become overwhelming, and you may lose sight of what you should be searching for. You will need to find some way to draw up a family tree, however basic.

There are numerous ways to do this. From simply scribbling a rough outline on a piece of paper to hiring a calligrapher to construct a beautifully drawn tree, it is a matter of personal opinion and taste. The research team involved with *Who Do You Think You Are?* used Family Historian (Version 2.1.6), one of the numerous computer programs available, to organize their research. Many of these packages are very easy to use and display your information in a way that is simple to read. Alternatively, on the Internet there are websites that offer templates for you to download to your desktop. There is no need to proceed in a systematic way at the beginning; just find the way of organizing your material that suits you best. As you go along, you will discover the method most suitable to your approach.

While on the subject of the Internet, it is worth bearing in mind that a huge amount of information exists on the web. There are countless sites dedicated to genealogy and family history. For beginners, most of these are baffling and impenetrable, and you may find they are as likely to turn you off, vowing never to become involved with family history again, as they are liable to set your genealogical juices flowing. As your quest progresses, there are several ways in which the web can act as a useful cross-referencing tool, or as a way of searching for information on specific events or eras, or for getting in touch with other family historians.

< **Olivia Newton John's maternal grandfather was Max Born, a German physicist who won the Nobel Prize in 1954 for his work in the field of atomic theory.** >

> There are websites that offer templates for you to download to your desktop.

< **It has been claimed that Prince Charles is a descendant of Viovide Vlad Dracula, aka Vlad the Impaler, aka Dracula. Let's hope that when he becomes king he doesn't follow Vlad's habit of inviting people to feasts, asking them to name previous rulers of Transylvania, and then impaling on spikes those who couldn't answer, watching them die in excruciating agony, decapitating them and feeding them to crabs. Must be tempting, though.** >

> For beginners, many websites are just as likely to turn you off as they are to set your genealogical juices flowing.

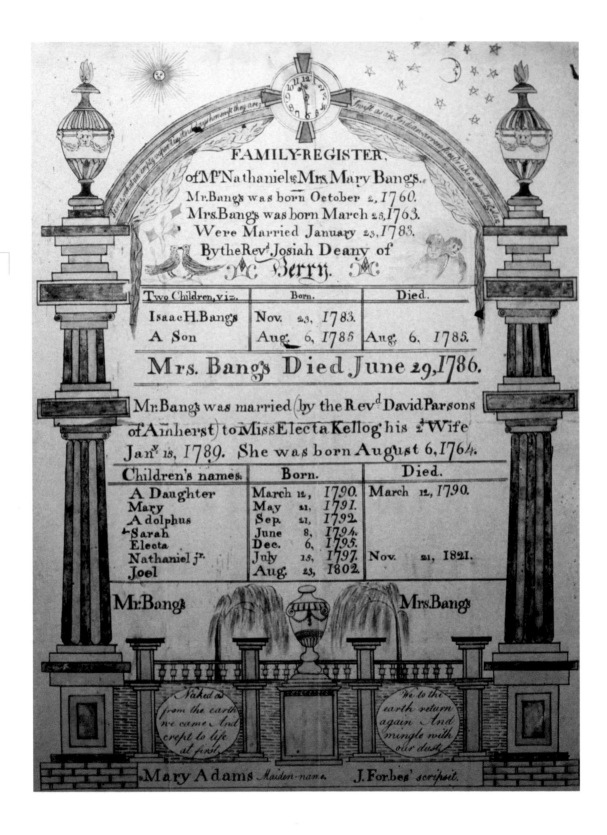

opposite: A family register such as this is invaluable, and may influence where you begin your search.

However, other than 'Googling' your name – typing it into a search engine and seeing what the results are for the sheer hell of it – beginners are advised to approach the Internet with caution at this stage.

With the information gathered from your relatives, and the clues you may have gleaned from any records and artefacts they passed on to you, it is time for the detective work to start in earnest. It is at this point that it is worth considering how you are going to approach your search. If your objective is to seek out one branch of your family, or even one person, your goal and method are clear. But if you are looking to draw up a family tree, even a limited one, it is a good idea to decide which branch of your family you will start to trace first. It is assumed you will start with yourself. You probably bear the same surname as your father. Your mother's maiden name opens up another avenue for investigation. Let's say you have the

details of your grandparents: that's four names in total to research. By the time you reach your great-grandparents there are eight names to look into – it is extremely time-consuming and you will have a lot of information to juggle.

It is far easier to start with one branch and take that as far as you can go, then return to the start and select another branch. Most beginners start with their father's family, the paternal branch. Of course, you may choose to investigate your mother's side instead. This may be the case if you have valuable documents from your mother's side of the family, or if your mother's maiden name is more distinctive than your own family name. The more unusual a surname, the easier your quest will be. If, for example, your father, John Smith, married a Hilda Heckerslike, the branch to explore first is obvious.

Did you know?

< **When Elton John changed his name from Reginald Kenneth Dwight by deed poll in 1972, he gave himself the middle name Hercules.** >

MOIRA STUART

As the BBC's first black newsreader on national radio and television, **MOIRA STUART** is not only experienced and highly respected but also one of Britain's most recognizable faces. Despite her celebrity status she has always kept a low profile, but Moira's fascination with her heritage persuaded her to let cameras follow her journey as she explored her family background.

Moira wanted to know more about how her ancestors have contributed to her sense of identity. She says she has always felt 'global' – rumours of Carib and Cape Verdean blood circulate in family legend. Certainly, the story of her family is characterized by remarkable movement and change.

It is a narrative that incorporates epic themes of migration, civil rights and colonialism; it ranges from the teeming metropolis of nineteenth-century London to the islands of the Caribbean, from English convent schools to the wilds of the Scottish Highlands. Ultimately it stretches back to Africa, beyond the barbarous transatlantic slave trade that claimed so many millions of black lives, uprooting countless people over centuries.

Moira's mother Marjorie was born in Dominica in 1921, just three years before the family moved to Bermuda. Her parents – Trinidadian Dr Edgar Fitzgerald Gordon, and his Dominican wife Clara – separated when Marjorie was a young girl. In 1935 she and her three sisters were sent to England to attend La Sagesse convent school in Hampshire. (Their two brothers, Teddy and Kenneth, remained in Bermuda until 1944, when they also left to study in Britain.)

PARTICULARLY FOR MARJORIE, the youngest girl, it was a major upheaval to be separated from her mother and to find herself in a strict boarding school, in a colder, less welcoming environment. Black faces in 1930s' Britain were treated as a rare and exotic sight, both inside and outside the school.

On completing their education at La Sagesse, the Gordon girls were sent to France for further studies, but returned to England when war broke out. After training as a nurse, Marjorie met and fell in love with a Barbadian lawyer, Harold Stuart. They married in 1943 and subsequently moved to Edinburgh, where their daughter Sandra was born. However, the marriage ended when Moira, their second child, was only a baby.

Edinburgh had already featured in the family's history three decades earlier. Marjorie's father, Edgar, had studied medicine at the university there. A high achiever, he had arrived in Scotland from Trinidad as a teenager in 1912, after a three-week voyage, and lodged with a local family. There were few black students at the university at that time, hardly any of them female.

Clara Christian was one. She had been at convent school in Edinburgh (her mother died when she was eleven), then had studied music at the prestigious Oberlin College in Ohio, USA, before following her father's wishes that she become a medical student. She was halfway through her course when she fell in love and married Edgar, in 1917.

Edgar's fortunes had taken a downturn when his father's livery business was decimated by the motor industry. So Clara gave up her studies and used the

subsidies from her father to support her new husband. The Hon. George James Christian was extremely displeased when he learned of his daughter's actions. Years passed before they were reconciled.

Edgar qualified in 1918 and accepted a job in the Scottish town of Kingussie, near Inverness. Few doctors wanted the post because of its sheer isolation. Edgar and Clara by then had a one-year-old daughter, Barbara, and in Kingussie twin girls, Joyce and Evelyn, were born. There are no records of the Gordon family in the town, but it is likely that Edgar practised at a hospital for TB sufferers – the Highland air was considered an excellent remedy.

Having served his internship, and after a brief

above left: Moira's mother and father, Marjorie and Harold Stuart.
above right: Moira's great-grandfather, George Christian.
middle: Marjorie and her sisters sailing for England, 1935.

visit to Trinidad, by 1921 Dr Gordon was beginning his career in his wife's birthplace, Dominica, where he secured the position of Chief Medical Supervisor. Their children Marjorie and Teddy were born there. However, this was not to be their final home. They moved on once more, this time to Bermuda, where their last child Kenneth was born. Dr Gordon became increasingly involved in Bermudian politics and stood as a Member of Parliament, motivated to challenge the racism he had witnessed both in England and in the Caribbean.

He went on to become a leading activist and fought strongly for the rights of Bermuda's workers. He was the founding father of the Bermuda Workers Association and played a major role in protests when black citizens were excluded from the civic commemoration of Queen Elizabeth II's coronation tour in November 1953.

Dr Edgar Gordon died in 1955, by then a central character in Bermudian politics. He is not, however, the only significant historical figure in Moira's family. Her great-grandfather, Clara's father, was another.

George James Christian was born in Dominica in 1869 and became a school teacher. With ambitions to be a barrister he travelled to London in 1899 and enrolled at Gray's Inn. His associates included a like-minded Trinidadian law student, Henry Sylvester Williams, who had founded an association concerned with promoting and protecting the interests of those of African descent, particularly in the British colonies.

When in July 1900 Sylvester Williams organised the landmark First Pan-African Conference, held over three days at Westminster Town Hall, G. J. Christian was one of the 30 delegates from Africa, the United States and the Caribbean who gathered in London to discuss ways of improving the conditions of black people everywhere. His speech 'Organized plunder and human progress have made our race their battlefield', dealing in part with the treatment of black people in South Africa where the Boer War was being fought, was reported at length in *The Times*.

George was called to the bar in June 1902. That same year he migrated to the British colony of the Gold Coast (now Ghana), where over the following decades he built up a successful legal practice in the town of Sekondi, naming his home 'Dominica House'.

His other Dominican daughter, Maud, after training as a midwife in Edinburgh at the same time as Clara was there, later moved to the Gold Coast, to join her father and his new African family. Although he maintained links with the Caribbean and made visits back to the island of his birth, he established a permanent and lasting connection with West Africa. He became increasingly involved with local life and politics, was Liberian consul for 30 years, and served on the Legislative Council until his death in 1940.

George Christian's political activism was undoubtedly kindled by an awareness of the history of his Caribbean ancestors, who had suffered the deprivations and indignities of enslavement. His father George senior, a school teacher, was born in Antigua within a few years of the abolition of slavery in the British Empire in 1834, though his exact date of birth is not known. Moira hoped to discover more about those earlier generations.

Researching slave records presents many challenges, particularly where enslaved Africans were given only first names, their surnames merely identifying their owners. On Antigua there was a white plantation-owning family called Christian, and circumstantial evidence points to a probable relationship with Moira's forebears.

In the Antigua National Archives Moira was able to study at first hand the registers of slaves that are the only remaining records – simple lists of the human property of their masters, which make grim reading.

Based on the 'Christian' surname, and the fact that Moira's ancestors gained an education soon after slavery was abolished, the likelihood is that this branch of her family were the descendants of white as well as black Antiguans.

Black faces in 1930s Britain were a rare and exotic sight.

HATCH, MATCH AND DISPATCH

SO HOW ARE YOU GOING TO TRACE YOUR ANCESTORS? BY LOOKING AT THE TRACES THEY LEFT. NO ONE, PARTICULARLY DURING THE PAST 150 YEARS, WENT THROUGH THEIR LIFE WITHOUT LEAVING SOME RECORD OF THEIR EXISTENCE. THE TASK IS TO FIND THESE CLUES, TO KNOW WHERE TO LOOK. THE BEST AND MOST OBVIOUS PLACE TO START IS WITH BIRTH, MARRIAGE AND DEATH CERTIFICATES, ALL OF WHICH ARE INDISPENSABLE AND RELIABLE SOURCES WHEN YOU ARE CONDUCTING A SEARCH.

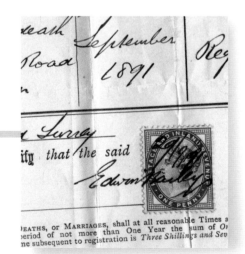

THE NATIONAL SYSTEM of registration of births, marriages and deaths started on 1 July 1837. Before then it was the law that people be christened, married and buried by the Church of England. These events were recorded in parish registers, which are examined later.

By virtue of the existence of birth, marriage and death certificates, it is much easier to trace a family back to 1837 than it is to go beyond that date. Tracing back to 1875, when it became compulsory to register the three events, is even easier. Yet even though registration was the law, this does not indisputably mean you will be able to find your ancestor's certificates. Some people, though remarkably few, slipped through the net. There were a variety of reasons why people were missed, but it was mainly those who were suspicious of why the state wanted such information and refused to give it, despite there being fines for non-compliance. Another way of upsetting the system was to give completely false details.

Once your search is under way, be aware that the system was not infallible and that occasionally the birth certificate of a much-sought great-grandparent may not exist. If this is the case, it is best to remember one important fact: don't panic! There is a way around most problems.

The information gleaned from your surviving relatives can be used to further your quest. The next step, for those with the time and the means to do so, is a trip to the Family Records

Prince William's birth certificate. Note father's occupation!

Centre in London. (If you are unable to make it to London – once again, don't panic. There are other ways of obtaining the same information without having to venture to the mean streets of the capital.)

FAMILY RECORDS CENTRE

Muslims have Mecca and Catholics have the Vatican: genealogists, meanwhile, have the Family Records Centre (known simply as the FRC by its regulars). Among family historians this unassuming building in a quiet, unheralded part of London generates as much excitement as Disneyworld does in children, and inspires as much awe as Lord's does in cricket fans. To say it contains a wealth of information is a bit like saying the Louvre has a few pretty pictures on its walls.

The truth is that anyone who is serious about tracing their ancestors should pay at least one visit to the FRC if possible (for tips on getting there, and opening times, consult the centre's excellent website www.familyrecords.gov.uk/frc). It houses indexes for every single birth, marriage and death recorded in England and Wales since 1837, as well as details of every available census from 1841 on microfiche, and electronic versions of the 1881 census and the 1901 census online. There is also the register of adoptions since 1927, Nonconformist parish registers and, for those still wondering if Great-uncle Hugo left them a few quid when he exited stage left, several resources for finding and looking at wills. And it's free to use, six days a week. Make a few well-planned visits to the FRC and it is entirely possible that you will have traced many of your ancestors back to around 1837.

Did you know?

< A Californian psychologist, a Professor Nicholas Christenfeld, conducted a study that revealed that an embarrassing surname can shorten your life. >

One word of warning, however: because the centre has such a mass of essential information, it can be very busy, on Saturdays in particular. There are many indexes and not a vast amount of space in which to browse through them. Instances of 'index rage', in which people clash when trying to reach for the same file, are not unknown. Judicious use of the elbows and a stubborn willingness to guard one's territory are vital.

The building has three floors. The basement houses a cafeteria, but the food and drink comes from vending machines, so either bring your own food or wander into nearby Exmouth Market where there are plenty of places to eat and drink. This floor is also where you find lockers in which to keep your belongings. The indexes for birth, marriage and

death certificates are on the ground floor, as are the adoption registers and the reception where you can ask for help from the knowledgeable and friendly staff and collect pre-ordered certificates. The tills where you queue and place your order for certificates are also situated here. The top floor is where the information from all the censuses is kept, together with several computer terminals that offer access to the Internet and a number of genealogical resources.

Our search starts on the ground floor among the births, marriages and deaths (BMD) indexes. Each is colour-coded: the birth indexes are red, marriages are green, and deaths, somewhat appropriately, are black. The filing system for all three is the same: the section for each index is arranged chronologically to the

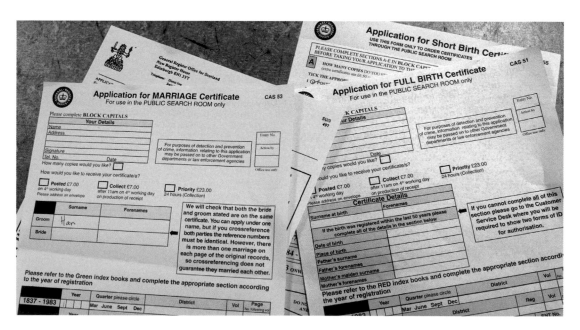

THE **NAME** GAME

IT CAN BE DISCONCERTING TO BE TOLD THAT YOUR SURNAME MAY NOT ALWAYS HAVE BEEN SPELT THE WAY IT IS NOW. BUT IT IS A FACT THAT FAMILY HISTORIANS HAVE TO BEAR IN MIND.

You must detach yourself and not be over-protective about how your name is spelt because you may find that a hundred or so years ago the spelling was completely different. Local dialect, intonation, an inability to spell, or simple embarrassment at a name mean it may have been recorded in a variety of ways.

For example, John Daker might have been so called in the 1850s, but by the turn of the century his children might have changed it to the more modern Dacre.

It might also have been misspelt on a birth certificate as Daycar, or some similar variation. Names change, and family historians have to recognize this if they are not to reach a dead end. Before visiting the FRC it is worth writing down every way your surname could possibly be spelt, allowing for spelling mistakes, phonetic spellings and other human foibles. For example, if your surname begins with an 'H', you need to consider the fact that the initial might have been dropped on the certificates of some of your ancestors. 'Harvey' might easily have been written down as 'Arvey'.

present day. Each year is divided into four quarters, labelled March, June, September and December, and each quarter is divided alphabetically by surname. The system is simple. Let's say, for example, that you are looking for a man named Dixon Carmichael, born in February 1912. Your first step is to go to the birth index section and find the right year. Then, when you have found the right shelf, find the file for March 1912 (which contains the first three months of the year) that corresponds to the initial of the surname you are looking for – in this case 'C'. Once you have found the file, pick it up and lay it before you on one of the desks – if there is space – and see if you can find the birth of a Dixon Carmichael. With a name like this there should not be too many. There is a chance he may not be there. Not everyone was registered immediately at birth, or even soon afterwards. His next of kin may

not have registered Dixon for six weeks or so, until April of 1912, which would explain why he is not in the March 1912 file. So your next step is to look in the 'C' file for June 1912 and see if his name is there.

It is often the case that you will have only a rough approximation of the date of a birth, marriage or death. If so, you will have to consult the files around the estimated date. Once you know what you are looking for and have familiarized with yourself with the system, and if you have above average eyesight, it is possible to scan files quickly and flick through the years. Some of the files are quite heavy – particularly those from the early years, pre-1865, where all the entries are written by hand. Sometimes you will not have even an approximate date, in which case it helps if you are researching an unusual surname.

When you find the name you are looking

< **When the 1901 census went online in January 2002, the server crashed immediately under the weight of 1.2 million eager amateur family historians across the world searching for their ancestors.** >

for, make a clear note of all that you see on the page. For Dixon Carmichael, the index reference to his birth may look like this:

CARMICHAEL Dixon Finch Leeds 9a 412

The first column is your ancestor's name. The second – and this is contained only in birth indexes after September 1911 – is his mother's maiden name; the third is the district where his birth was registered. This is the local area registry or county registry, and is not always exactly where someone was born. It is a good idea to have some knowledge of the towns and boroughs surrounding the place where the birth you are searching for took place, especially if the surname is a common one. The final two columns correspond to the volume and page in the register.

You need to write down all the information in the index entry, together with the quarter and year of the file you discovered it in – June 1912 in this example. This last detail is very important. There is nothing more frustrating than spending hours lifting files and scouring them, then finding your elusive ancestor and scribbling down everything in the reference, only to forget which file you found him in – a vital detail that you will need to order the certificate. It may be that you will have to plough through all the files once again until you discover the one in which you found your ancestor.

Once you have the information you need, it is time to order the certificate. At the front desk, pick up an application form for the type of certificate you require and fill it in. The forms are pretty self-explanatory. It may be the case, especially with common surnames, that there is more than one candidate to be your ancestor in that quarter, in that district, in that year, with that name. If so, you can request that the name

NET NOTE

If you cannot get to the FRC, there is a wonderful resource on the Internet featuring searchable indexes of all Births, Marriages and Deaths from 1837 to 2002 at https://www.1837online.com/Trace2web/ Searching is simple: select the event (birth, death or marriage); select a date range, the maximum being ten years; then type in the first three letters of the surname for which you are searching. There is a charge to view the pages you require; £10 will buy, for example, 122 units. Viewing a page incurs the cost of one unit.

be 'checked' against points that you supply. For example, if you are searching for the birth certificate of Samuel Smith it is very likely there will be more than one 'hit'. If you have any further knowledge about the Samuel Smith you are searching for – his father's name, perhaps – you can enter this in the 'checking points' on the back of the form. When your order is submitted, the certificates that correspond to the index references you supplied will be checked against the points you gave. So if you know the name of Samuel Smith's father was Algernon, the references will be checked against this detail. If a corresponding certificate is found, it will be sent to you; on the other hand, if there isn't one, nothing will be sent and you will still be liable to pay the £4 checking fee. Occasionally, there will be times when you have no 'checking points' and determining which is the right Samuel Smith will be problematic. The

option then is to delay your order and find some more information on the person you are searching for, perhaps from a marriage or death certificate or the census returns. Most family historians have endured the frustrating experience of ordering a certificate that turned out to be the wrong one.

If you are certain you have the right person and index reference, the main decision you will have to make is whether to pay (at the time of writing) £23 to receive the certificate the next day; £7 to collect it after four working days have elapsed from the time of ordering it; or the same price to have it delivered by post, which takes around ten days. Then you take the form to the tills, hand over the cash, sit back patiently and wait for the past to open up.

< British surnames, with few exceptions, derive from four categories: surnames based on the first name of an ancestor (e.g. Andrew, Samuel); surnames recording localities or places where ancestors originated (e.g. Scott, Barnes); surnames recording the occupation or status of the ancestor (e.g. Smith, Clark); and surnames that are nicknames, describing the ancestor's temperament, face, morals, etc. (e.g. Keane, Small). >

TOP TEN **BMD INDEX** TIPS

1 Gather as much information as possible about a person before you look.

2 If you are prone to absent-mindedness, it can help to make a note of the index years and quarters you have checked during your search in case you are interrupted, or suffer a case of 'index brain' – a little-known, yet catastrophic, genealogical condition where all indexes merge into one and you can't remember where your search started or where it has got to.

3 Some files are under repair. Make a note of any that affect your search and come back to them later.

4 Remember that someone might not have been registered until several weeks after they were born or died, so their name may not be in the same quarter as their precise date of birth/death.

5 As soon as you find the person you are looking for, note down clearly: the quarter and year of the file, for example, June 1912; their full name, for example, Dixon Carmichael; their place of birth/marriage/ death, for example, Leeds; the volume reference, for example, 9a; and, finally, the page number, for example, 412.

6 If the surname is a common one, you may find more than one candidate in a file. In this case, the district of birth may help you to single out the person you want. Ask the staff or consult the maps on the wall to discover the volume numbers for different parts of the country. The current volume number for Leeds, for example, is 9a.

7 Early volumes are handwritten and often difficult to read. Consult a member of staff or, if you are bold, a fellow researcher.

8 If you are looking for when a person was married, but don't know the year, work backwards from when they had their first child, or any known child, year by year until you find the date of the marriage. Just hope the details you have aren't for the last child of 17!

9 To confirm you have the correct marriage in indexes for before 1912 – when the names of both spouses were first recorded – note down the district name, reference number and page, then look for the husband's or wife's name elsewhere in the index (the bride will be entered under her maiden name) and confirm it is the same.

10 Be aware that the spelling of names changes over time.

IAN HISLOP

AS EDITOR OF THE satirical magazine *Private Eye* and ever-present on *Have I Got News For You*, Ian Hislop has become the *bête noir* of the political and media establishment, revelling in pricking the pomposity of the great and the good. Think of Ian Hislop and the first thing that comes to mind, other than his famous 'If that's justice then I'm a banana' response to his magazine losing a libel case, is him dishing out caustic one-liners on Friday night TV.

It is clear from his editorials and TV appearances that Ian has his conservative side and, despite possessing a healthy scepticism towards people in positions of power, in many ways he could be described as 'establishment material'. This is probably a consequence of his family history. Ian grew up enjoying the privileges of post-colonial life; he attended a traditional public school and flew to various foreign countries – Nigeria, Kuwait, Saudi Arabia and Hong Kong – to join his civil engineer father David and his mother Helen for holidays. He has fond memories of them dressed in swimming costumes on beaches and boats or in formal evening wear going to balls and receptions. Despite the travel, the exotic lifestyle his parents enjoyed and the obvious benefits that were bestowed upon him, the peripatetic way of living left him with little sense of 'roots', other than being aware that his father was Scottish and his mother was from Jersey, and that both left their small communities behind them. Finding out about the past and tracing the path of his predecessors enabled Ian to gain some sense of his family's journey.

THE FIRST PORT OF CALL was his mother, Helen Rosemarie Beddows. From her Ian feels that he has inherited some important attributes: she was highly literate, good at crosswords and Scrabble, and 'that endless inventive wordy stuff' as he describes it. He was keen to discover more about her – she died a few years ago – not least because she grew up on Jersey and was there when the Channel Islands were occupied by the Nazis in 1940. His mother rarely talked about this, but then the occupation of the Channel Islands is one of the least elucidated moments of the Second World War. The facts are simple enough. Faced with the prospect of the Germans occupying the islands, the British government decided they could not be defended. Residents felt they had two options: to try and evacuate to the mainland, an opportunity seized by thousands; or to stay in their homes and take their chances under the Nazis. Ian's mother's family bravely took the latter.

Helen Rosemarie was 11 in 1940 and lived with her parents in St Helier. Her lifelong friend, Iris Le Feuvre, still lives on Jersey and remembers life under the Germans. The aftershock of the occupation is still felt now, more than half a century after its end. People were accused of collaborating with the Nazis; some felt the islanders could have done more. Others fought back with acts of defiance like Iris's family who hid an escaped Russian prisoner of war from the Germans and sheltered and fed him throughout the occupation. For Ian's mother and her friends getting by meant struggling to find food, clothing and an education but as teenagers it was also important that life went on – a fondly remembered youth club ensured that young people could still foxtrot and whist drive their way through the war. People struggled to make ends meet whilst desperately hoping that the Nazis would be defeated and life in Jersey would return to normal. This hope became fervent after 1942 when orders came through that 2000 people were to be deported and interned. Top of the list were Jews, ex-servicemen and those born on the mainland. The day the British were deported, a crowd of people went down to the harbour to watch the ship depart. As the deportees sailed away the group on the shore struck up a chorus of 'There'll always be an England' – an act that landed some of them in prison. From across the waves they could hear the deportees joining in. Helen Rosemarie's cousin was one of those shipped off, but her father, William, was ignored by the Nazis, even though he was a veteran of the Boer War. As he was in his sixties, with a gammy leg, it is possible that they assumed he was no longer a threat.

William had joined the second battalion of the King's Own Royal Lancaster regiment in 1895. The medals he earned while fighting in South Africa are held in the regimental headquaters in Lancaster and locate him in five major campaigns of the Boer War. Perhaps the most famous of these is the battle of Spion Kop (incidentally, this battle gave its name to the famous Spion Kop – known more commonly as 'the Kop' – at Anfield, the home of Liverpool FC) where he and his regiment were in the thick of it. Apart from William Beddows, there were other significant witnesses to the battle, one of the bloodiest and most futile of all those fought in the 1899–1902 war: Winston Churchill was a 23-year-old war correspondent and described the five days of fighting as 'among the strangest and most terrible I have ever

above: Ian's mother, Helen Rosemarie Beddows.

witnessed'; and Mahatma Gandhi was a stretcher bearer, the experience confirming him as a life-long pacifist. Hundreds of British soldiers died trying to hold a hill in the face of relentless shelling by the Boers, with little cover. Ian has visited the battle site and seen the place where so many men died. The Royal Lancasters suffered heavy losses in the battle, and the awful sights William Beddows must have witnessed would have stayed with him until his death. Yet it did not prevent him signing up in 1906 for a further ten years' service, though as a sergeant in Jersey his life was far less eventful.

Ian knew much less about his father's family history. His grandfather, David Murdoch Hislop, was raised in Ayr. Ian knew he had fought in the First World War, but other than this he was an enigmatic, distant and mysterious figure in Ian's early life. He was a headmaster, and a strict one at that, a church deacon and a stern moralist. Finding out what happened to him in the war might go a long way in helping Ian to understand this complex character. It emerged that he volunteered in 1915 but did not make it to the front until the beginning of 1918 at the earliest (his service records, like those of so many others, were lost in the blitz of the Second World War.) However, a postcard sent to David Murdoch Hislop by a French soldier he met during his participation in the liberation of Clary in October 1918 gives evidence of his partici-pation. He was part of the 9th Highland Light Infantry that fought at Targelle Ravine on 29 September that year. His regiment suffered grievous losses during one morning of fighting for little gain. They fought for two solid weeks before breaking through the front line, and for two days after the battle the regiment's remnants (now at quarter strength) were billeted in Clary. During this time the battalion band put on a concert to raise morale in the troops. Perhaps experiences such as these explain how the men could endure such horror. David Murdoch Hislop certainly seemed to find succour in his beliefs, and there is no reason to believe he had any loss of faith at any time during the conflict.

In 1922 he married a Catherine Matheson, whose family history offers yet another fascin-ating military story stitched into Hislop legend. Ian's great-great-great-grand-father was a Murdo Matheson, a private soldier in the 78th Highland Regiment. Despite his low rank, his career was remarkable: he joined up in 1794 and fought in many colonial campaigns, including battles at Assaye in India and in Java. While they are not as famous as Trafalgar and Waterloo, they were certainly instrumental in forging Britain's global empire.

The colonel of the regiment was Lord Seaforth, a Scottish aristocrat. He gained immense prestige by raising a regiment and was paid handsomely for it, too. His recruits came mostly from among those who scraped a living on his estate and signed up for fear of losing their homes. Each household felt duty-bound to provide a soldiering son, of which Murdo Matheson was one. He turned out to be a true survivor, finally leaving the military life at the age of 45 in 1813. Amazingly, Ian discovered that Murdo Matheson was among the first wave of British troops to invade South Africa. How strange then that 100 years later Ian's maternal grandfather, William Beddows, would spend the early years of his life defending that very same land.

above: Ian's grandfather, William Beddows.

She was literate, good at crosswords and Scrabble, and 'that endless inventive wordy stuff' as he describes it.

OUT AND ABOUT

It may be that you are unable to make it to the FRC. This doesn't mean you cannot find the certificates you require. You could visit your local births, marriages and deaths office, but beware – this will not be a place to browse. To find and order a certificate you will need specific details – approximations won't do. And you can obtain certificates only for the area covered by the local office.

Another, perhaps easier, option is to go to a major library that holds the BMD indexes on microfiche. Find the reference you require and make a note of it. You are then presented with three options for obtaining the certificate: either by post from the General Register Office (GRO), by phone, or, only if you live in the UK, online. The first two options will cost you £8.50 (£24.50 if you want the certificate as a priority and dispatched the next working day). For details of addresses and phone numbers visit www.statistics.gov.uk/registration. The third option, ordering online, is relatively new and, at £7 and £23 respectively, is a cheaper option. You will need to give your credit or debit card details, your full name and your postal and email addresses, as well as the details of the certificate you are looking for.

Of course, this option is fine if you know the exact registration details. If you don't, the GRO will conduct a search for a certificate without a specific reference for an additional £11.50, regardless of how you order. The more information you send, the more chance staff will have of finding the right certificate, so full names and exact dates and places are helpful. Spending as much time as you can finding the references you need at the nearest library that houses the BMD indexes will reap dividends.

< Karl Marx applied for naturalization in 1874 but was turned down after recommendations by the Metropolitan Police that he was the 'notorious German agitator, head of the International Society and an advocate of Communist principles'. >

YOU CAN'T ALWAYS **GET** WHAT YOU WANT

FAILING TO FIND A NAME THAT OUGHT TO BE IN THE INDEXES? HERE ARE SOME POSSIBLE REASONS WHY YOUR SEARCH ISN'T THROWING UP THE PERSON YOU ARE LOOKING FOR.

1 A family member may insist that an ancestor came from one part of the country when they were in fact born and raised in another. Keep an open mind and be prepared to accept that what you have been told may be wrong.

2 The person you are searching for might have been born in hospital. This could have been situated in a district different from the one in which they lived.

3 Clerical error. Civil registration records are as prone to mistakes as other sources: the person's name could have been spelt wrongly or their age misheard.

4 Human nature. Perhaps due to mistrust of authority, or for a variety of other reasons, some people simply avoided being registered or gave false information to the registrar.

BIRTH CERTIFICATE

Birth certificates are essential sources because of the quantity of information they contain – they offer information that you simply cannot find anywhere else. They can also act as building blocks in your search. Once you have one, it is possible to obtain a marriage certificate. From this you can obtain more birth certificates and so on.

From left to right the form gives: the date of birth (day, month and year) and place of birth (street name, the name of the town, village or hamlet); the next two columns are taken up by the name and sex of the person born; then comes the name and surname of the father. If the child is illegitimate, this column is left blank. The next one features the mother's name, surname and, a real bonus for family historians, her maiden name. Next comes the father's occupation, then the name and residence of the informant (in most cases the mother).

Often during the early years of registration, when illiteracy levels were high, you will see a cross, the mother's mark, in this column. The last three columns are of little interest to us. Two deal with when the birth was registered and by whom, and there is a final column headed 'Name entered after registration', which is seldom filled. See page 21 (bottom) for an example of a certificate of this kind.

So a birth certificate will tell you where a person was born, where they lived, who their father was, what he did for a living and the maiden name of their mother. Armed with this information, you can work backwards and search for a marriage certificate of the parents in the years before the birth, using the most unusual of the two surnames as your search focus, and then cross-referencing it against the other one to confirm you have the right marriage.

Did you know?

Playboy creator and ageing, leather-faced lothario **Hugh Hefner is a direct descendant of William Bradford, the first governor of the pilgrims who arrived on the *Mayflower*, the founder of the Plymouth colony and a Puritan to boot. Other celebrities with ancestors on the *Mayflower* include Stephen King, Humphrey Bogart and Marilyn Monroe.** >

[PAGE 69]

1889. MARRIAGE solemnized at the Parish Church, in the Parish of Saint Clement Danes, Strand, London, in the County of Middlesex.

No.	When Married.	Name and Surname.	Age.	Condition.	Rank or Profession.	Residence at the time of Marriage.	Father's Name and Surname.	Rank or Profession of Father.
137	August 27th 1889.	Herbert Edward Tarver	31	Bachelor	Secretary to a Public Company	Savoy Hill House	Edward Tarver	Banker's Clerk
		Emily Dorothea Hartley	31	Spinster		St. Leonards Terrace Chelsea	Henry Hartley	Gentleman

Married in the Parish Church, according to the Rites and Ceremonies of the Established Church, by _____ or after Banns, by me,

F.I.H.S. Pennington M.A. Rector

This Marriage was solemnized between us, { Herbert Edward Tarver / Emily Dorothea Hartley } in the Presence of us, { Emily C. Long / Edward Tarver }

I Certify that the above is a true Copy of an Entry in the Register Book of Marriages in the Church of Saint Clement Danes, in the County of Middlesex. AND I FURTHER CERTIFY that the said Register Book is now lawfully in my custody. WITNESS my hand this 27th day of August, 1889.

Book No. _____ F.I.H.S. Pennington Rector.

By the 14 & 15 Vict. c. 99, sect. 14, a Copy of any Book which is of such a public nature as to be admissible in evidence on its mere production from the proper custody, is made admissible in evidence in any Court of Justice provided it *purport to be Signed and Certified as a True Copy* by the officer to whose custody the original is intrusted. *In re Hall's Estate, 22 L.J., ch. 177, and re Porter's Trusts, 25 L.J., ch. 88, it was held that Extracts from Parish Registers of Baptisms, Marriages, and Deaths, purporting to be signed, some by the "Rector," some by the "Vicar," some by the "Incumbent," and some by the "Curate" of the Parishes, were receivable in evidence—the Court considering that each Incumbent was an "officer to whose custody," &c., within the meaning of the above Act. By the 52 Geo. 3, c. 146, s. 5, the Register Book of Marriages, Baptisms, and Burials, is placed in the custody of the Rector, Vicar, Curate, or other officiating Minister. By the 23 Vict., c. 15, the adhesive stamp is to be obliterated by the person signing his name or initials thereon, together with the date of the day and year on which he shall write the same.

(Add to Signature the word Rector, Vicar, Curate, or Officiating Minister, as the case may be).

MARRIAGE CERTIFICATE

Reading left to right, a marriage certificate offers the following information: date of the marriage; full names of the bride and groom; their ages (if an entry says 'of full age' it probably means over 21, though not always!); their 'condition', for example, whether they were a bachelor, spinster, widow or widower; their professions; their addresses at the time of marriage; their fathers' names and surnames (if relevant, the word 'deceased' or an abbreviation thereof appears next to the name/s); and their fathers' professions. Below this you can find information on where the marriage took place, who officiated at the ceremony, and who the witnesses were.

Marriage certificates can put rocket boosters on your search. Let's say, for example, that you have used your grandfather's birth certificate to discover the names and surnames of your great-grandparents (and the maiden name of your great-grandmother). From the ages on their marriage certificate (if the precise ages are recorded) you can calculate the years in which both people were born, allowing you to search for and obtain their birth certificates. The certificate may also reveal that one or the other was a widow or widower. To whom were they first married and how did their spouse die? You can disappear back to the marriage indexes and see whether the widow or widower's name appears in the years preceding their marriage to your great-grandmother/father. That will then lead you to another marriage certificate, giving you the name and age of the deceased spouse. Then you can wade through the death indexes to discover how and when this person died.

DEATH CERTIFICATE

Reading left to right, a death certificate provides the following details: date and place of death; name and surname of the deceased; their sex; their age; their occupation; cause of death; signature, description and address of the person who informed the registrar of the death; when it was registered; and the name of the registrar.

Death certificates provide an extra piece of genealogical information: age at death, which is essential if you are seeking to make a complete family tree showing dates for when each person was born and died. They are also fascinating if one of your ancestors died young and you want to know why. Apart from satisfying simple morbid curiosity, a death certificate has its practical uses, for example, as an alternative should either a birth or marriage certificate prove elusive. For instance, I could

not find a marriage certificate for my great-grandfather, Thomas Waddell, and this was preventing me from unearthing his date of birth. I knew he had married a Maria Goldsmith Harrison because they were both on my grandfather's birth certificate of 1907. But a search of the marriage indexes produced nothing. From the oral history I had gathered of my grandfather's family, I knew his youngest

of Death.

Cap. LXXXVI., et Anno Primo Victoriæ Reginæ, Cap. XXII.

is,

Croydon _____ in the Counties of *Croydon and Surrey*

Rank or Profession	Cause of Death.	Signature, Description, and Residence of Informant.	When Registered.	Signature of Registrar.
Bankers Clerk	Gastro Intestinal Catarrh & Congestion of Liver Cardiac Syncope Certified by H. J. Strong. M.D	Sarah Tarver Widow of deceased present at the death 4 Alexandra Road Croydon	Twenty-eighth September 1891	Edwin Bailey Registrar

Croydon _____ in the Counties of *Croydon and Surrey*

DEATH REGISTER, Entry No. 379 _____ And I further Certify that the said

Edwin Bailey Registrar.

September 1891

RING OFFICER, and SECRETARY, who shall have the keeping for the time being of any REGISTER BOOK OF BIRTHS, DEATHS, or MARRIAGES, shall at all reasonable Times allow Searches to be made ries in the same, on payment of the Fee hereinafter mentioned; (that is to say,) for every search extending over a period of not more than One Year the sum of *One Shilling*, and *Sixpence* E." (Including the Stamp the " Certificate " is *Two Shillings and Sevenpence*,) thus the cost of a Certificate at any time subsequent to registration is *Three Shillings and Sevenpence*.

brother was born around 1920, and that Thomas Waddell died shortly afterwards. So I went to the death indexes and started searching for Thomas's death from 1920. In 1922 I found a record of the death of Thomas Waddell in Morpeth, Northumberland, the area in which my grandfather was raised. The age given was 52. I ordered the death certificate and returned to the birth indexes. In 1870 I found a reference to his birth certificate. I also knew that my great-grandmother, Maria Waddell, née Harrison, died a few years after the birth of my father in 1940. In 1943 I found a reference to her death at the age of 67. This allowed me to find the birth certificate of Maria Goldsmith Harrison in 1876. My search, previously stalled by the lack of a marriage certificate, was back on track.

NET NOTE

WWW.

One of the best and most popular sites on the Internet for people searching for ancestors is at http://freebmd.rootsweb.com. Transcribed by volunteers, it boasts free, searchable indexes to births, marriages and deaths between 1837 and 1983. More than 80 million records are on the database and it is growing constantly. Coverage is better for some years than others, so searching can be a bit hit and miss. But it costs nothing to search, and the results can be immensely rewarding. The site shouldn't be relied upon as a primary source – mistakes can be made in transcription – but as a cross-referencing tool and a way to further your search in the comfort of your home, it is unsurpassed.

OTHER REGISTRIES

Your ancestry may not originate in England or Wales; it could be Scottish or Irish. In which case you may wish to pay a visit to the registries of these nations either to start or continue your search. Here is brief guide to accessing and using the information their archives hold.

Scotland

If you have Scottish antecedents, you will have an advantage over your English and Welsh counterparts because, although civil registration did not start until 1855, it was kept far more thoroughly. All certificates feature more information, too. Birth certificates, for example, contain not only all the details shown on English ones, but also the date and place of the parents' marriage. This marvellous addition saves masses of time, allowing you to go straight to the

*Note that, where available, Scottish birth
certificates give the place and date of the
parents' marriage.*

marriage index and find the correct union without any need to rifle through the files. It gets better: Scottish marriage certificates carry the names of both the bride's and the groom's parents, rather than just names of the fathers. Death certificates also feature the mother's and father's names – unlike English and Welsh certificates, which show neither. This all saves the family historian a lot of time.

In 1855 the certificates were even more detailed: birth certificates showed the ages and birth places of the parents and the number of siblings, living and deceased; marriage certificates gave details of any previous marriages; and death certificates offered place of birth, details of marriages and all living and deceased brothers and sisters. Sadly, this bureaucratic largesse lasted only a year because of the amount of work involved in maintaining it.

All records are held by the General Register Office at New Register House, Edinburgh. Unlike at the FRC, a fee is required to search. You will be required to pay £17 for a day and £10 for an afternoon. But it is worth it. All the indexes are on computer, which at the very least prevents 'genealogist's elbow' – a consequence of hulking great files around at the FRC. You can also get a lot more done in one day. If you have the correct reference, you will be able to inspect the original records on microfilm or microfiche, and write down the details or photocopy them (you can also order copy certificates by post). This allows you to conduct several searches in one day and get quite far back into your family's history.

A couple of points to bear in mind. First, it is advisable to call ahead and book a seat and terminal if you will have to travel any distance; second, you are only allowed to use pencils, so make sure you stock up beforehand.

If you are unwilling or unable to travel to Edinburgh, fear not: there is a searchable index at the General Register Office website. Bear in mind that, out of respect for the living, only birth and death certificates more than 100 years old – 75 years for marriage certificates – are available for browsing. You also have to pay £6 to access the records.

Ireland

General registration began in Ireland in 1864. At the General Register Office in Dublin there are no consolidated indexes; the records for each county are filed separately. The certificates offer virtually the same information as their English and Welsh counterparts, apart from death certificates, which offer only the person's name and age, and the date and place of their death.

As elsewhere, original records are not open for inspection. Instead, you will have to find the correct reference, then request, for a small sum (just under 2 euros), a photocopy of the original entry to check it is the one you want before ordering a certificate. As in Scotland, this system allows family historians to go back through several generations simply by noting the details on the photocopy and continuing from there.

Northern Ireland

Following the partition of Ireland in 1922, all records pertaining to Northern Ireland are held at the General Register Office of Northern Ireland in Belfast. The office offers a distinctive system to researchers: users can conduct either an assisted or an index search. The former, which costs £21, involves the assistance of a member of staff. An index

Did you know?

< **Elvis Presley's genealogy can be traced back to American President Abraham Lincoln. Actor Tom Hanks is another who counts Abe among his ancestors.** >

All these archives provide a postal service if you have sufficient information and send the correct fee. For birth certificates you need the full name of the person, and their date and place of birth, as well as the names of their parents. After 1911 you also require the mother's maiden name for English and Welsh certificates. For marriages you need the date and place of the marriage, the full names of both spouses and, if possible, the name of each father. Death certificates require the full name of the deceased, together with their place and date of death. Consult the appendix for addresses, websites and phone numbers.

ADOPTION

search is, as the name indicates, a solo search through the indexes and costs £9. When you have the reference you require you can ask a staff member to check it for you – they will read out the info and you can note it down. It is worth booking ahead for both methods.

Isle of Man and Channel Islands

For those with relatives from the Isle of Man or the Channel Islands, both boast registries that are open to the public. The Isle of Man records, held in Douglas, date back to 1878. For the Channel Islands, civil registration commenced in 1840 in Guernsey, and two years later in Jersey.

There were no such things as adoption certificates until 1920, and the records held at the FRC do not start until 1927. The indexes give only the adoptive name of the child and their adopting parents. There is no record of the child's name before adoption. The certificates are similar to birth certificates – they give the correct date of birth, for example. Close relatives of the mother, such as aunts and uncles or grandparents, sometimes adopted illegitimate children, but the certificates do not divulge this information. Only an adopted adult can obtain the original copy of his or her birth certificate.

ILLEGITIMACY

THERE IS NOTHING NEW ABOUT ILLEGITIMACY. EVERY FAMILY HISTORIAN IS LIKELY TO ENCOUNTER IT AT SOME POINT, UNLESS THEIR ANCESTORS WERE UNDERSEXED OR PRACTISED IN DECEPTION. THE WORD 'BASTARD' HAS BECOME TABOO BECAUSE OF ITS PEJORATIVE CONNOTATIONS. PREVIOUS GENERATIONS WERE NOT SO SHY. BASTARD WAS A RELATIVELY COMMON SURNAME, AND WAS DERIVED FROM PEOPLE WHO LITERALLY WERE.

Over time there have been fewer incidences of the name, which was either changed completely or altered to B'stard. **The Victorians – who else? – were the first to become queasy about illegitimacy,** and it was during this hypocritical era, which coincided with the era of civil registration, that all the steps to prevent it becoming known were taken. Sex was not something that happened in polite society – there were 60,000 prostitutes in London and Paris who catered for that sort of thing. Of course, scandal still occurred: it was not uncommon for servants of the landed and middle classes to become pregnant by the son or father of the house, or for employees to have illegitimate children by their boss. However, they found themselves out on their ear if they did.

Illegitimacy presents problems for the family historian; **on a birth certificate it is likely there will be a blank where the father's name should be**, ruling out a possible line of research. It can be worth checking the marriage indexes shortly after the date of the birth to see if the couple married to 'legitimize' the child.

Close relatives might have adopted an illegitimate child and it is worth checking census returns to see if this is the case. Many children grew up unaware that their much older 'sister' was their mother, and their 'parents' were actually their grandparents. All this is worth bearing in mind when the presence of illegitimacy enlivens your family history.

PUTTING YOURSELF FIRST

IT MAY BE THAT YOU HAVE NO LIVING RELATIVES AND ARE FORCED, FOR WHATEVER REASON, TO START FROM SCRATCH. HERE IS A QUICK, STEP-BY-STEP GUIDE TO GETTING UP AND RUNNING.

1 Retrieve your birth certificate, which will give your parents' names or, at the very least, your mother's maiden name.

2 From this work out an approximate date of marriage and obtain the certificate.

3 Among other things, this will give your parents' ages and the names and occupations of their fathers – your grandfathers.

4 From the marriage certificate calculate the respective dates of birth of your mother and father, and obtain a birth certificate for whichever branch of the family you wish to pursue.

5 This birth certificate will give you the names of your grandparents. Return to step 2.

The Abbey register of the marriage of the Duke of York (later George VI).

PAGE 60 B

...3. Marriage solemnized at *Westminster Abbey* in the *Close* of *St Peter Westminster* in the County of *Middlesex*

When Married.	Name and Surname.	Age.	Condition.	Rank or Profession.	Residence at the time of Marriage.	Father's Name and Surname.	Rank or Profession of Father.
26th April 1923	Albert Frederick Arthur George Windsor	27 Years	Bachelor	Prince of the United Kingdom of Great Britain and Ireland Duke of York K.G. G.C.V.O. K.T.	Buckingham Palace	George Frederick Ernest Albert Windsor	H.M. King George V of the United Kingdom of Great Britain and Ireland and of the British Dominions beyond the Seas Defender of the Faith Emperor of India
	Elizabeth Angela Marguerite Bowes-Lyon	22 Years	Spinster	—	17 Bruton Street W.	Claude George Bowes-Lyon	Fourteenth Earl of Strathmore and Kinghorne

...ried in *Westminster Abbey* according to the Rites and Ceremonies of the *Established Church* by *Special License* by me,

This Marriage solemnized between us,

Albert
Elizabeth Bowes Lyon

Randall Cantuar.

in the presence of us:—

Cecilia Strathmore & Kinghorne *Strathmore Kinghorne*

George R.I.   *Edward P.*   *Arthur*   *Herbert E. Ryle (Dean)*
Henry.

Mary R   *A. Bonar Law*   *W. Brechin: Primus*

Alexandra R   *Cave*   *Cambridge*

Daisy...   *William C Bridgeman C.J. London:*   *Athlone.*

Portland   *George*   *Louise Prs. Royal*   *House...*
Slamis
Mary   *Victoria.*   *Michael. B. Lyon*   *David B. Lyon*

MEERA SYAL

MEERA SYAL GREW UP in the mining village of Essington in the West Midlands, a place she once famously described as 'a cross between *Twin Peaks* and *Crossroads*'. The contradictions of growing up in modern Britain with immigrant Asian parents, and of living between two cultures, are ones Meera has explored hilariously and successfully in her work, particularly in her novel *Anita and Me*. One of the most respected writers and comedians in Britain, she also wrote the novel *Life Isn't All Ha Ha Hee Hee*, the screenplays for *Bhaji On The Beach* and *Anita and Me* and the script for the musical spectacular *Bombay Dreams*, as well as co-writing and appearing in comedies such as *Goodness Gracious Me* and *The Kumars at No 42*. Cultural issues underpin Meera's work; yet this was the first time she had taken an in-depth look into her family history and searched for what she describes as her rebel roots.

Meera's parents both originate from the farmlands of the Punjab in north-west India. Meera's father, Surendra Syal, hails from a small village called Lasara. Indian ancestry is difficult to trace through documents such as birth certificates but family records are kept at shrines in holy cities around India. In the ancient city of Haridwar on the banks of the Ganges, a Hindu priest is responsible for preserving the genealogy of the Syals in a book called a Bahi. Names of family members are added to the Bahi after they die. From this book Meera discovered that the Syals have been living in Lasara for the past 250 years.

THE SYALS originally come from Lasara but Surendra grew up in 1930s Lahore, where his father Tek Chand Syal had gone in search of better prospects. As a student at the D.A.V. College in Lahore, Tek Chand became involved in the student demonstrations against the British. Some of these were peaceful protests but others were not and he was forced to disappear temporarily from Lahore in the early 1930s. But in 1936 he returned from hiding to begin his career as a journalist at *Milap*, an Urdu newspaper at the vanguard of the Indian Independence movement.

With the struggle for independence from Britain won in 1947, the Partition of India was a high price to pay. India was forcibly split in two according to religion – Pakistan, with its majority Muslim population, became an Islamic republic and India, with its Hindu majority, a secular republic. During Partition 12 million people were uprooted from their homes and over a million people were killed in communal rioting between Hindus, Muslims and Sikhs. Soon after Partition, trains carrying the butchered bodies of the victims began arriving on both sides of the border, as revenge and retaliation permeated a blood-soaked Punjab.

Punjab was carved in two and so bore the brunt of the division. The Syals, like millions of other Partition refugees, were forced to flee. Tek Chand decided that Pakistan was not a safe place for his Hindu family and moved them to Delhi while he stayed behind. For the next few months Tek Chand was trapped in Pakistan and could not find anyone willing to take him across the border. Over in Delhi his family feared him dead, yet another victim of Partition. Eventually a Muslim horse-and-cart driver agreed to make the perilous journey and Tek Chand made it to India alive. Unfortunately, the driver did not make it back to Pakistan. He was found dead, a victim of Hindu youths seeking revenge for the murder of one of their own.

Deeply affected by these atrocities and disillusioned by the post-Partition politics of the Congress Party in India, Tek Chand became a staunch Communist after Independence. In the late 1940s, he and other Communist Party of India members set up a pro-Communist newspaper called *Savera*. But after only eight months a lack of funds forced the paper to close. Moving on to another Urdu newspaper *Tej*, Tek Chand became a much-respected journalist, active in the trade union movement, and a passionate defender of workers' rights.

Meera's mother's side of the family displayed rebel roots too; her grandfather, Phuman Singh, marched with hundreds of other Sikhs during a struggle against the British in the village of Jaito in the Punjab. The series of marches began after the

top left: Phuman Singh with his daughter, Surrinder Syal.
top right: Tek Chand Syal with his wife Susheela Syal.
middle: Surrinder and Surendra.

British raided a Sikh temple in Jaito and interrupted the reading of the Guru Granth Sahib (the Sikh holy book), an act that the Sikhs considered sacrilege. For two years, between 1923 and 1925, the Sikhs embarked on a non-violent political-religious campaign against the British, marching in groups of 500 or more from Amritsar to Jaito, hundreds of miles across the vast Punjab. This protest is commonly referred to as the Jaito Morcha (Jaito Agitation). Phuman Singh, Meera's grandfather, participated in the 11th Jatha, which set off from Amritsar in July 1924 and arrived in Jaito in early September 1924. Up to 20,000 Sikhs were arrested during these marches, including Phuman Singh, who spent more than a year in prison. In 1972 he was awarded a Freedom Fighters Pension for his part in the Jaito Morcha. This contribution is acknowledged in the *Who's Who of Punjabi Freedom Fighters*, a book recording those Punjabis who struggled for independence from the British.

Phuman Singh was also an atypical Jat Sikh landowner. Leaving his agricultural background, he became something of an entrepreneur as the owner of a number of businesses. Although the father of three daughters in a society that favoured sons, he proudly considered his daughters the equal of any male. Unusually for the time, he educated all three of his daughters, including Meera's mother Surrinder. At school, Surrinder excelled as a sportswoman and also expressed an enthusiastic interest in drama.

It was whilst studying at college in Delhi in the 1950s that Surrinder met Surendra, Meera's father. They were from different religious backgrounds – Surrinder was a Sikh, Surendra was a Hindu. Nevertheless, they fell in love and for seven years they met at famous landmarks around Delhi, including India Gate and Lodhi Gardens. When her parents suggested searching for a suitable husband for their daughter, Surrinder told them that she had already chosen the man she wanted to spend the rest of her life with. At first Phuman Singh objected to Surrinder's choice of husband on the basis of religion, but in time he embraced his son-in-law. Very much in love, Surendra and Surrinder married in Delhi in 1958.

In 1960 Surendra left India for England to pursue his education in London. His journey to England involved a 17-day boat trip from Bombay to Europe, followed by a train journey across Italy, Switzerland and France, and then a ferry to Dover. Like many other Asian immigrants at the time, he arrived at Victoria Station with little money in his pocket. At first he lodged at a bachelor boarding house in Swiss Cottage, North London, but when Surrinder joined him soon after the two of them moved to a larger flat close by. Education had been the reason for their journey to England but Surrinder soon fell pregnant with Meera and Surendra had to abandon his academic pursuits in order to support his family. Isolated and lonely in London, Meera's parents moved to the West Midlands to be closer to Indian friends who had also recently arrived from India and were already part of a vibrant and burgeoning Indian community.

Meera was born in the early sixties in Wolverhampton. When she was one, her family moved to Essington and later, after she won a scholarship to an all girls grammar school, they moved to Walsall. Meera grew up during a time when Asian immigration was developing into a contentious issue in Britain. In 1968, Enoch Powell delivered his infamous *Rivers of Blood* speech in nearby Birmingham, warning against the dangers of Commonwealth immigration to Britain. Throughout the 1970s and 1980s the Asian community cemented their position in British culture, against obstacles of hostility, racism and discrimination. Meera's own work and position reflect a deep-rooted Punjabi heritage in a contemporary British setting.

Tek Chand decided that Pakistan was not a safe place for his Hindu family.

MAKING SENSE
OF THE CENSUS

THE FIRST CENSUS WAS TAKEN IN 1801, FOLLOWING DECADES OF
ARGUMENT ABOUT WHETHER ITS INTRODUCTION CONSTITUTED AN
INTRUSION OF PRIVACY. FOR SOME PEOPLE THE VERY IDEA WAS AN
INFRINGEMENT OF HUMAN RIGHTS, A SIGN OF AN OVERMIGHTY
EXECUTIVE ABUSING ITS POWER. WHETHER GENEALOGISTS EVER
FOUND THAT THESE OBJECTORS WERE DIRECT ANCESTORS OF TODAY'S
DAILY MAIL READERS IS UNKNOWN. BUT THE ARGUMENT IN FAVOUR
OF SOME FORM OF CENSUS WAS CONCEDED BY THE TURN OF THE
NINETEENTH CENTURY, AND IN ENGLAND AND WALES, THE CHANNEL
ISLANDS AND THE ISLE OF MAN A CENSUS WAS CARRIED OUT IN 1801
AND ONE HAS BEEN CONDUCTED EVERY TEN YEARS SINCE, EXCLUDING
1941 BECAUSE OF THE SECOND WORLD WAR. THAT FIRST CENSUS
REVEALED THAT 9 MILLION PEOPLE LIVED IN THOSE ISLES.

> " The first three censuses of
> 1801 to 1831 are of no value
> to the family historian. "

UNFORTUNATELY, that is all it revealed. The first three censuses of 1801 to 1831 are of no value to the family historian. All the enumerators conducted was a headcount of the population; no names, ages or addresses were recorded out of respect to the privacy campaigners. By the late 1830s the debate had become heated. The argument was now over how detailed the questions should be. Things haven't changed a great deal. Even now, after 200 years and 20 censuses, there are still those for whom the idea of the state gathering information about its citizens is an anathema. In the last census in 2001, there was a group of people with far too much time on their hands – more commonly known as students – who attempted to encourage people, when asked about their religion, to give the answer 'Jedi', on the basis that if a certain number were recorded as being 'Jedis' it would become a recognized religion. 'Jedi Knight' now has its own census code.

Rag Week pranks like this were not on the minds of our ancestors as the 1841 census approached. It was agreed that more detailed questions could be asked, though there were some limits. Names could be recorded for each household, but their relationship to the head of the household could not; children under 15 had their precise ages recorded, while those aged 15 and above had theirs rounded down to the nearest five; questions about the profession or trade of the head of the household followed. Finally, citizens were asked whether they were born in the same country they lived in, or in Scotland, Ireland or 'foreign parts'.

The head of the household fills out census forms in 1901.

The 1841 census of England, Wales, Scotland and Ireland was the first to be taken by the General Register Office, and can be seen as a trial run. Ten years later the kinks had been ironed out and, thankfully for our purposes, more information was recorded. The census now gave everyone's place of birth, precise age and relationship to the head of the household, making it prime source material for us. (In 1891 and 1901 a further category was added: people had to admit whether they were (1) deaf and dumb, (2) blind, or (3) lunatic, imbecile or idiot.)

A day or two before census night – held in June in 1841, either March or April ever since – forms were distributed to the head of the household, usually the father or senior male. A few days later enumerators returned to collect the forms or give assistance to those unable to read or write. Once the questionnaires had been completed and collected, the data was entered into books, records that survive to this day.

A census is a snapshot in time. It reveals where your family was living and with whom on the night it was taken. Just pray that your great-great-grandfather did not decide to go on a three-day drinking jag the night he got the form, and fail to return or come round until all the forms had been collected. By using and interpreting census returns we can pick up clues about how our ancestors lived, the conditions they lived in, exactly where they lived, track them every ten years to see if they

Hundreds of women compile information from the 1901 census.

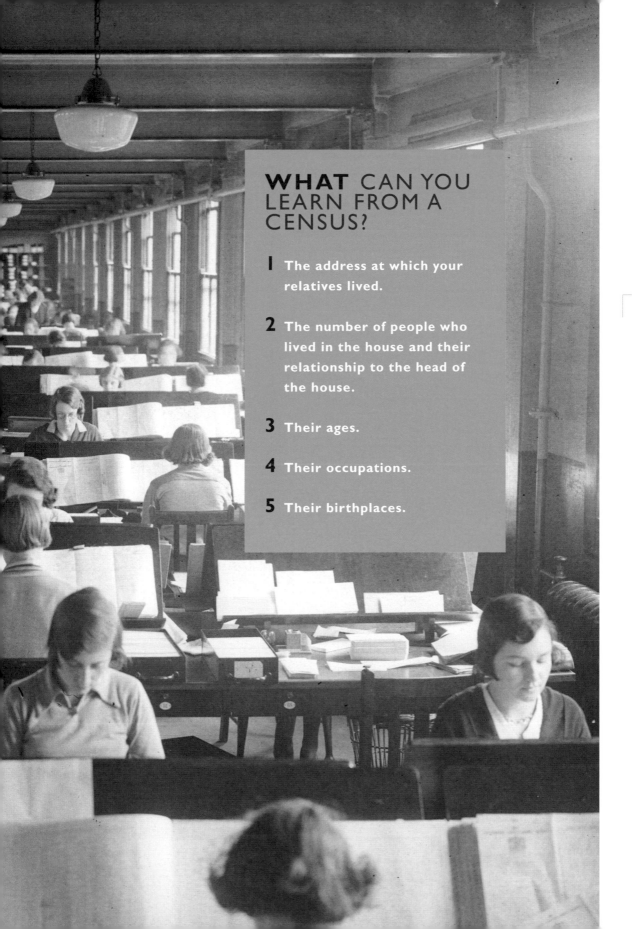

WHAT CAN YOU LEARN FROM A CENSUS?

1 The address at which your relatives lived.

2 The number of people who lived in the house and their relationship to the head of the house.

3 Their ages.

4 Their occupations.

5 Their birthplaces.

Civil Parish	Ecclesiastical Parish	County Borough, Municipal Borough, or Urban District	Ward of Municipal Borough or of Urban District	Rural District
of *Lambeth (part of)*	of *St Pauls W Brixton* (part of)	of *Lambeth (part of)*	of *Stockwell (part of)*	of

Cols 1	2	3	4	5	6	7	8	9	10	11	12	13
No. of Schedule	ROAD, STREET, &c., and No. or NAME of HOUSE	HOUSES In-habited	Uninhabited In Occupation	Not in Occupation	Building	Number of Rooms occupied if less than five	Name and Surname of each Person	RELATION to Head of Family	Condition us to Marriage	Age last Birthday of Males	Females	PROFESSION OR OCCUPATION
291	90 Ferndale Rd Contd						Caroline Richards	Wife	M		44	
							Emily J B "	Daur	S		22	Milliner
							Thomas G "	Son	S	19		Commercial Clerk
						✗	Sidney A "	Son	S	17		Stockbrokers " Co
292	92 " "	1					Thomas H Cotton	Head	M	48		Solicitors " Law
							Annie Jane "	Wife	M		35	
							Marguerite A "	Daur	S		15	Millinery Apprentice
							Violet May "	Daur	S		14	Dressmakers Assistant
							Thomas W "	Son	S	12		Oilmans Assistant in spare
							George N "	Son	S	11		
							Dorothy R "	Daur	S		9	
							Nellie "	Daur	S		7	
							Annie B "	Daur	S		3	
							Henry C "	Son	S	2		
						✗	Charles S James	Lodger	M	50		Drapers Assistant
293	94 " "	1					John W Jackson	Head	S	17		Music Hall Artiste
							Rose "	Sister	S		12	" " " Act
							Stephen "	Brother	S	8		" " "
							Willie Jackson	"	S	2		" " "
							Eliza Goff	Servt	M		38	Domestic Servant
							Joseph Popock	"	S	17		Music Hall Artiste
							Arthur Williams	"	S	14		" "
							Maurice	"	S	12		" "
							Daniel Murphy	"	S	16		" " " Ac
							James Cawley	"	S	13		" " "
							Charles Chaplin	"	S	12		" " "
294	96 " "	1				✗	Allen Diggens	Head	M	35		Carpenter Bench
							Amelia "	Wife	M		45	
							Harriet M "	Daur	S		11	
							Allen F "	Son	S	8		
							John A "	Son	S	6		
3	Total of Schedules of Houses and of Tenements with less than Five Rooms	3						Total of Males and of Females...		19	12	

NOTE.—Draw your pen through such words of the headings as are inapplicable.

The 1901 census return for Mr Charles Chaplin:
note how much information the return contains.

moved, died or simply vanished, and use the information to trace our roots further back in time.

1901 ONLINE

The latest census we can get our hands on is for 1901. This is because censuses are protected by the 100-year-old rule to safe-guard the confidentiality of the living. Given that the 1901 census is the latest available, and is the most accessible because it is fully transcribed and available on the Internet, it is a good place for any beginner to go to early on in their search, allowing them to 'break through the 1901 barrier'. A census can simplify and amplify your search – by giving you the age of a person on a certain date it allows you to calculate their birth date and obtain a birth certificate without having to follow an elaborate paper trail.

The 1901 census on the Internet at www.census.pro.gov.uk is easy to use. Be aware, though, that it is by no means infallible: the database you are searching is a transcription of the original, and the hand-writing on this will not have been easy to read. Place names, where people were born in particular, are commonly misspelt. Be warned also that a search can take a long time if it produces a lot of results – if this is the case, you may get the dreaded, rather schoolmarmish, response, 'Your search is taking too long'. Also,

computers do crash, and you will have to pay to view the records you find.

That said, it is still worth it. You are given a choice between Person Search, Advanced Person, Place, Institution, Vessel or Direct Search. Help for each is available on the site. The most popular is the Person Search. It is obvious that the more information you possess, the easier it is to locate the ancestor you are searching for. If you are looking for James Smith and know little about him other than his name, sex and the general region where he lived, it will be like trying to find a needle in a large stack of needles. Your search will return hundreds of results, and you have no way of knowing which of them is the one you want. If, however, you know that James Smith was born in 1888 and was therefore either 12 or 13 in 1901, that his birth place was Dorking and that he lived in the same area, the result may well be in single figures; and by looking at

the people he lived with, you may be able to identify, beyond doubt, the James Smith you are searching for. If the name isn't a hugely common one, it is wise to start with a broad search and narrow it down if you get too many results; the detailed information you have may not accord with what has been entered on the census, and by being too defined you might miss the person for whom you are searching.

Once you have completed your search and worked out which result you want, you can pay to see a transcription of the person's entry and, if you then choose to do so, transcriptions of all the other people in the household. These will cost you 50p. You can download the original census image, on which you will be able to see everyone who was in the house on census day (though you must have Acrobat Reader to do so). This allows you to save the image on your hard disk, print it out, zoom in and out for a better view, and generally use it

< Bald star of *The King and I* Yul Brynner was related to bloodthirsty slayer of millions Genghis Khan. In the film *Taras Bulba* Yul got to play his ancestor. >

CENSUS
WORKING
OVERTIME

HERE ARE SOME HANDY TIPS TO USING THE 1901 CENSUS **ONLINE**.

1 For a Person Search, start broad and narrow down the options if you get too many results.

2 If you know both a person's forename and middle name, use the Advanced Person Search because the initial Person Search does not recognize middle names.

3 If you cannot decipher the original census image, try reversing the colours to see it white on black. This can make it easier to read.

4 If yours is a casual search over the course of a few days or weeks, use vouchers rather than paying by credit card.

left: The Registrar General, Mr Michael Reed, searching the archives at Somerset House in 1966.

as you please. The only drawback is that it is sometimes difficult to decipher the original handwriting.

Some people bridle at being asked to pay to access the census records, but for others it is a small price for the convenience of accessing them through their home PC. There are two ways to pay: by credit card or by voucher. The minimum payment in both cases is £5, which will allow you to see ten entries. Vouchers are available from the Family Record Centre, the Public Record Office (now named the National Archives), the Society of Genealogists (see appendix) and other family history societies. The benefit of these is that they can be used over a six-month period from the time they are first registered. There are also no issues of security if you are unwilling to divulge your credit-card details over the Internet. Ludicrously, a credit-card payment is valid for only 48 hours, meaning that the scope for

casual, occasional browsing is limited. However, if you are in a position to put in a few hours of searching and expect to obtain results, a credit card is very convenient because you can sign up for more sessions there and then should your current one run out. You can also check to see how much you have spent and what money you have left. When you take a break, remember to suspend your session and not log off as doing so will prevent you resuming later.

But what can the information you find tell you? If the BMD certificates you have located take you back beyond 1901 and supply you with enough information to perform a detailed search, you will be able to see where the person or people you have traced lived at the turn of the century. For example, I knew my great-grandmother was born in 1890. I went to the 1901 census website and searched for Mary Quinn, entering her age – approximately 11 – in the search field and the keyword place

> If the BMD certificates you have located take you back beyond 1901 and supply you with enough information to perform a detailed search, you will be able to see where the person or people you have traced lived at the turn of the century.

below: The Family Records Centre is the genealogist's Mecca.

name, Alnwick, where I knew she had been born and raised. Given the amount of information I had, my search returned only one result. The correct one, too. It revealed that she had several brothers and sisters, all older than her, and that her mother and father, John and Mary Quinn, were both alive in 1901, and it told me how old they were on census night. Before I got too excited, however, the next revelation was that both John and Mary had been born in Ireland. To find out more about them I would have to try and discover how, when and why they came to England. Already the census had given me a starting point: their eldest child James Quinn was born in Alnwick around 1865. I later discovered a marriage certificate that showed they were married around this time. Up until this point I had wondered if they had left Ireland in disgrace, with Mary pregnant with James, but now I had evidence of their marriage I would have to

search for another reason for their emigration.

The next thing to do would be to check the available censuses before 1865 to see if either John Quinn or Mary Graley – her maiden name – were recorded as being in the Alnwick area. This would mean using the census returns either at the FRC or at my nearest county record office.

Did you know?

< **Walt Disney is descended from the Reverend George Burroughs, grand wizard of the 'witches' executed in Salem in the 1690s.** >

JEREMY CLARKSON

JEREMY CLARKSON HAS a reputation for straight talking. Whether railing in his newspaper column against the pernicious creep of political correctness, or wailing about the growing crop of speed cameras on our roads, as presenter of *Top Gear*, he favours the blunt, no-nonsense approach. Like most Yorkshiremen he prefers to brandish the broadsword rather than the rapier. So it was no surprise that when he was asked to present a programme about his family's history his response was abrupt: 'Too boring to bother with,' was the phrase he used, one learnt from his grandfather (a talent for scorn obviously runs in the family). Jeremy could not understand why anyone could possibly be interested in the lives of his ancestors.

Yet for a man who glories in the engineering achievements of Britain's past, who made a passionate plea in the recent BBC series *Great Britons* for Isambard Kingdom Brunel to be lauded as the greatest Briton, the revelation that some of his forebears played a significant part in the country's rapid industrialization during the nineteenth century was one to make him proud. The period is of special interest to Jeremy because he is in the process of writing a book about ground-breaking machines. He is fascinated by the Industrial Revolution, by British design and craftsmanship, and by how thousands of ingenious hard-working industrialists built modern Britain. To learn that his ancestors were at the forefront of these developments was exciting and immensely gratifying. It involved him going back to his Yorkshire roots and becoming embroiled in, and seeking to solve, a long-running family puzzle.

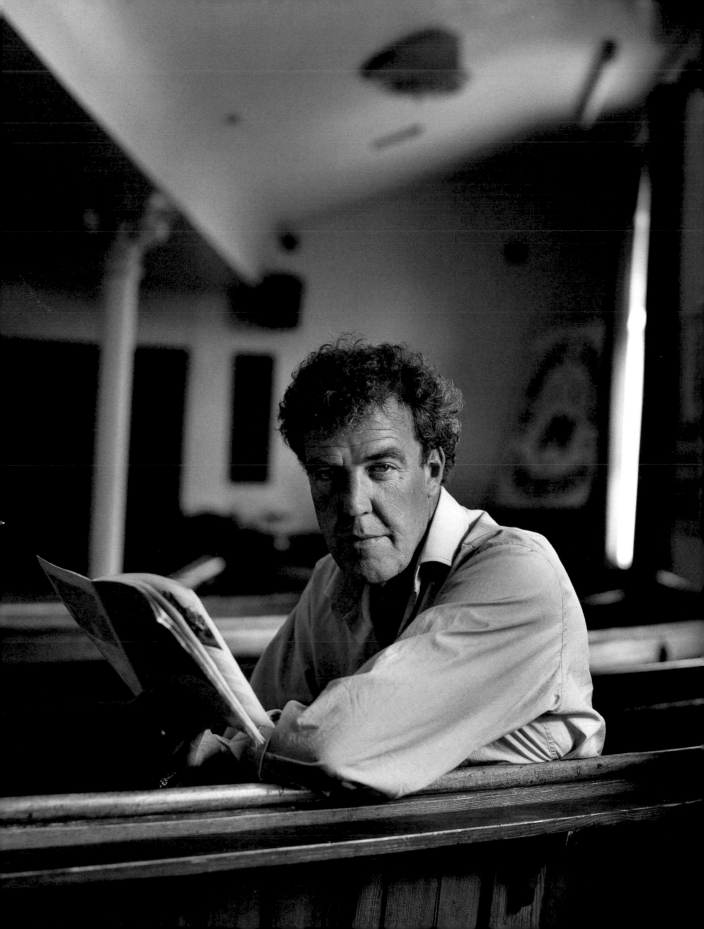

JEREMY WAS AWARE that one of his ancestors had invented the Kilner jar for preserving out-of-season fruit. The first of its kind – it was sealed with a tight-fitting lid and rubber band – it is used in homes today and still bears the family name. But he was unaware that the story of the Kilners, his maternal ancestors, was an amazing tale of rags to riches and back to rags. Family legend has it that, despite this invention, the Kilners became bankrupt. Jeremy's relatives told him there were rumours that the patent for the jar had been stolen by another firm, or that it had never been registered. Whatever the reason, which Jeremy was determined to uncover, had it not been for this mysterious reversal of fortunes he might have been born into extraordinary wealth, and never had to work his way up from local cub reporter to motoring journalist and TV personality.

The story starts with John Kilner (b. 1792), Jeremy's great-great-great-great-grandfather. He worked in a glass factory, and on a fishing trip with friends he spotted an ideal site for a glassworks. He duly set it up and made the step from employee to employer – a gigantic one in the early days of the Industrial Revolution. Through thrift and skill, John Kilner turned the business into a massive success: he soon possessed two huge factories, the first was in Thornhill Lees and the second in Conisbrough, both in Yorkshire. He picked an opportune time to open the Thornhill Lees factory, given that the legislation that taxed glass was repealed in 1845. Also, industrialization and growing prosperity had increased the demand for, and production of, glass jars and bottles. John died in 1857, and the firm was taken over by his four sons: George – Jeremy's great-great-great-grandfather – William, John and Caleb. Each learnt their trade on the factory floor, and the business, known by then as Kilner Brothers, continued to thrive and flourish.

Caleb, one of the brothers, was given the task of removing himself from the bosom of his family in Yorkshire and going to London to open a warehouse. From here Kilner glassware was transported all over the world. The Kilner brothers won the only prize medal awarded to British manufacturers of glass bottles at the Great International Exhibition in London in 1862; in the 1870s and 1880s they won medals and awards in Paris, Philadelphia, Sydney and Melbourne. The Kilners were at the summit of their trade.

But what happened? What of the rumours about the patent for the Kilner jar? It seems that the Kilners never lodged a patent for their jar, maybe because registering patents was costly and inefficient at that time. The answer had to lie elsewhere. Jeremy managed to obtain a copy of the firm's Jubilee brochure, and in it he found a clue that led him to discover that in the early 1870s the Kilners' neighbour in Thornhill Lees, a Lord Savile, took out an injunction against them because the smoke from the factory's chimneys was, or so he claimed, blighting his land and preventing him from creating a residential development. The free-holders, leaseholders and ratepayers of Thornhill Lees wrote a memorandum to him asking him to drop the injunction, as did the firm's workers, arguing that it would close the factory and ruin the town. Lord Savile ignored their protests. On 23 February 1872 an injunction was passed preventing

top left: George Kilner.
top right: Gwendoline and Robert's wedding day.
middle: George Knowles.

the Kilner Brothers glassworks at Thornhill Lees from operating until gas furnaces were installed. For six months the factory lay idle while the modifications were made. But rather than ruining the firm, it seems that the furnaces actually aided it by increasing production.

When Caleb Kilner died he left the equivalent of millions of pounds in his will, most of it to his son George and some to his son-in-law, Harry Smethurst. Records show that neither of them had much money when they died, and the question is: what happened to Caleb's millions?

It emerged that George was not much of a manager, and the firm declined under his control. But there might have been little he could do. Small family businesses were coming under increasing pressure from cheap imports in the early twentieth century, while others merged to survive. One example of such a merger was United Glass Bottle, a conglomeration of six glassware companies. It bought the Kilners' patents when the firm eventually withered and died. The business had been well suited to the nineteenth century, but the demands of the twentieth had been too much. Jeremy also found out that George Kilner had bought an expensive machine for the glassworks, but had struggled to meet the loan repayments.

Harry Smethurst, who married Jeremy's great-grandmother, Annie Kilner, did not work at the glassworks. He was an architect and designed many of the buildings in the pit village of Denaby, as well as many for the Kilner brothers. Rumour had it that he spent some of the money he inherited from Caleb on a motor car – in about 1901, which must have made him one of the first car owners in south Yorkshire. (Perhaps it was here

that the Clarkson love of motoring was first engendered?) The story goes that Annie was renowned in the village. Legend has it that mothers threatened recalcitrant children with her, saying they would send them to Annie to be sorted out if they did not behave.

The couple liked to show off their wealth, and may have frittered away much of the money they inherited. Some remained, but when Annie died she disinherited Jeremy's grandmother, Gwendoline, who did not get a penny. Jeremy's relatives had been told that Gwendoline had been cut off because she married beneath herself, which was not in keeping with Annie's view that her daughter should marry a wealthy man. In fact, Jeremy found out that when the factory closed there had been a family rift over how the proceeds of the closure should be divided, and Gwendoline may have sided with a cousin. She was estranged from her mother as a result, and the money went to her brother, Tom.

Gwendoline married Robert Livesey Ward, a local GP, who dedicated his life to helping miners after experiencing a colliery disaster at first hand when he was 12. In later life he wrote a book, *Old King Coal*, that was part memoir and part social commentary. He, like Harry Smethurst, was a car lover; he spent much of his life saving for a Bentley, only to become bored with it after a couple of years and eventually selling it.

By the end of his quest, Jeremy had discovered that the reason why he was not sailing on a yacht or retiring to his family mansion in the South Yorkshire countryside was due to several factors: George Kilner had not been the best boss; later generations had not planned for developments in the glass market; and the twentieth century had been tough on small family firms that refused to change. The achievement of the Kilners was nevertheless a huge one: the Kilner jar still exists today, a testament to the values of British design and craftsmanship. Perhaps most important of all, Jeremy learnt that ancestors can be anything but boring.

He might have been born into extraordinary wealth, and never had to work his way up.

BEYOND THE 1901 BARRIER

Only the 1901 census is on the Internet (though there are some sites that claim to have most of the 1881 and some of the 1891 censuses online). The only other complete census available electronically is that of 1881. This is searchable at the FRC and, taken in tandem with the 1901 census, it allows you to track people's movements between 1881 and 1901. If someone appeared in the 1881 census but not in that of 1901, it is likely they died at some point between the two. To narrow the search further, you can check to see if they were alive when the 1891 census was taken. Unfortunately, at the time of writing, this census, like those of 1841, 1851, 1861 and 1871, is not available electronically. While all census returns are available on microfilm, not all are on microfiche.

> The only other complete census available electronically is that of 1881.

CENSUS MISTAKES

YOU MAY NOT BE ABLE TO FIND YOUR ANCESTOR IN THE CENSUSES. HERE ARE SOME REASONS **WHY.**

1 Five per cent of the population don't appear in a census for one reason or another. For example, people who sleep rough.

2 People moved around more than we think in the Victorian era, but if someone should have been at a certain address on census night and wasn't, check the rest of the neighbourhood. Who knows, they might have gone round to friends for a drink that night and not made it home.

3 Between 5 and 10 per cent of the 1861 census is simply missing.

4 The enumerator might have misheard or misunderstood what they were told, so individual entries can be wrong: ages can be a year or two out, occupations can be inaccurate and birthplaces misspelt.

below: The census enumerator in a Gray's Inn Lane tenement in 1861.

Did you know?

< **The surname Kennedy, in its original Celtic, means 'ugly head'.** >

Personally, I hate microfilm. Scanning through endless reels of the stuff on badly lit screens coated in inches of dust, developing repetitive strain injury by having to rewind whole reels manually, threading crumpled, creased pieces of film over and not under the rollers – all of this is about as much fun as gouging your own eyeballs out with a teaspoon. Yet, like going to the dentist or travelling by coach, it is a necessary evil.

At the FRC, given the helpful staff and easy-to-understand filing system (well, easy once it's explained to you), using the microfilm systems is less harrowing than at other places. There are several explanatory leaflets, which are well worth reading, or alternatively ask a member of staff for a quick how-to guide.

The census returns are on the first floor of the FRC. In a nutshell, each census year has its own colour code: 1841, green; 1851, red; 1861, blue; and so on. You will need to know where your ancestors were living in whichever year you are looking at. The first step is to check whether there is a surname index for the place you are interested in. Instructions at the front of the binder will explain where to find this. If the place you want does not have a surname index – only the 1881 census has a complete surname index, and this is held on a database – check whether there is a street index for the place you are interested in.

There is every chance you won't be able to find the place in either the surname or the street index, so the next stop is the place-name indexes. These list every parish, town and village in England and Wales, and provide the name and number of the registration district and sub-district (note that in the 1841 census the number given in the place-name index is the page number). This will enable you to go to the correct reference book to find the piece reference for the film you want. Should you at

Personally, I think that using microfilm is as much fun as gouging your own eyeballs out with a teaspoon.

any point become confused or uncertain about what to do next, ask for help.

Once you have found the piece reference, collect a box-marker for the shelves. The markers have the numbers of microfilm-readers on them, so the one you pick up – C5, for example – corresponds to the reader you will be using. When you find the correct film in the cabinet marked with the year and reference number you want, replace the film with the marker. You are then free to look through the film at your leisure. There is nothing for it, I'm afraid, other than to spin through the census trying to find the person you are looking for. The joy comes when your neck is locked in place after hours of staring at the dimly lit screen, and your eyes are sore through straining to make sense of the barely legible scrawl – yet you find that elusive ancestor. Tempting as it might be to head straight to the pub in celebration, vowing never

to pick up a piece of microfilm again, please remember to put the film back.

Microfiche is a less traumatic prospect for the indolent. The files are indexed alphabetically for each census by surname and place, thus reducing the chances of a long, fruitless trawl. But they are by no means exhaustive. You may discover that there is no surname index for certain districts in certain years, in which case take a deep breath, count to ten and head for the microfilm indexes. If you are fortunate enough to find the surname index you require, find a microfiche-reader, collect the corresponding marker and insert it into the slot from which you took the index. Then you are ready to 'go ficheing'.

< **The legendary Cubby Broccoli, the man behind the James Bond films, claims he is descended from the family who developed the vegetable that bears his name. It was a cross between a cauliflower and a rabe.** >

CENSUS **LIES**

THE CENSUS IS NOT INFALLIBLE. PEOPLE DIDN'T ALWAYS TELL THE TRUTH. HERE ARE SOME OF THE MOST COMMON PORKIES TO WATCH OUT FOR.

For some women, time can be an elastic concept. You may find that a female who gives her age as 23 in the 1861 census might miraculously still be only 28 when the 1871 one was taken.

Birthplaces can be inaccurate. People often gave the place where they were brought up, or where they had spent most of their life. Sometimes they just didn't know where they were born, so simply made it up.

Children may be listed as scholars. This doesn't necessarily mean they were at school; they may have been working and their parents didn't want anyone to know this.

Tens of thousands of women earned their living by prostitution. Unsurprisingly, few admitted this to the census.

right: Tables of statistics being compiled from the 1931 census.

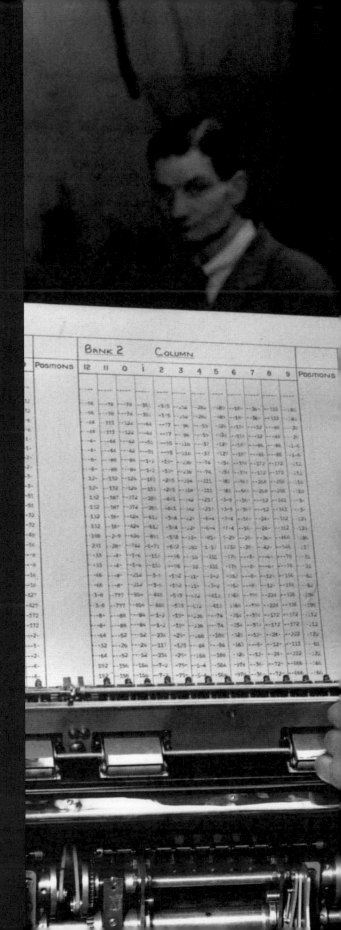

Did you know?

< In the first half of the nineteenth century, almost one third of all brides were pregnant when they got married. >

HIDDEN TREASURES

So we have the whole range of censuses to use. How can we use them? The fact is they provide far more information about our ancestors than birth, marriage and death certificates do. When you find your family members on a census return, look at the surrounding houses and buildings and see how many people were in each of them. This will give you a glimpse into the environment in which your forebears lived. Look at the occupations of other householders in the street; it was common for people engaged in the same type of job to live alongside each other. My father's family were coal miners, and in the areas where they lived they were surrounded by other mining folk, often with up to 12 people living under the same roof. The 1881 census revealed that my great-grandfather was working down the pit at the age of 12.

If you are seeking a thorough picture of your family, why not track them from 1841 to 1901? This will enable you to gain real insight into your ancestors lives, to see how their occupations and living conditions changed. Often the two went hand in hand. For those of you who are aiming to go way back in time, beyond the era of civil registration, the censuses will provide clues to the birth dates of people born before 1837. You can then pinpoint a date and place to aid your search when you come to look through parish records for mentions of christenings and marriages.

Censuses can be used for troubleshooting, to maintain momentum in your search, and to help locate that elusive ancestor who seems to have evaded any form of civil registration. I could not understand why my great-grandfather, Thomas Waddell, did not appear in

< To avoid the dreaded census enumerators on a point of principle, the author Agnes Strickland spent the whole of census night, 1871, in a cab being driven around the streets of Southwold, Suffolk. >

the 1901 census. Nor did his wife, Maria. I knew they were married by then because my father remembered an Uncle William who fought in the First World War, which meant he would have to have been born by around 1900 at the latest. I had birth and death certificates for both Thomas and Maria, but couldn't find a marriage certificate for them, even though I knew Maria's maiden name was Harrison. I had tried, or thought I had tried, every variant spelling of Waddell in the marriage indexes and the 1901 census.

So I turned to the 1881 census index database at the FRC. This is a wonderful tool because it will give you variations on the spelling of the name of the person you are searching for. I typed in Thomas Waddell and punched in his date of birth – in 1870 – and the area in which I thought he might have lived (Northumberland).

There was only one result that seemed to fit: a ten-year-old listed as Thomas Waddle (Wilson). The head of the house was a William Wilson. His wife was Mary Wilson. There were three children with the surname Waddle and three others named Wilson. This fitted with what I knew because Thomas Waddle's birth certificate (which spelt his surname as Waddell – an example of how inexactly names were spelt in those days; see 'The Name Game' on page 43) informed me that his mother's name was Mary, his father's William Waddell. But who was this Wilson character? The Wilson children on the census were the same age as some of the Waddle children, so there were obviously two different mothers. After a bit of head scratching it became clear that Mary had married William Wilson some time before the birth of Barbara Wilson, the youngest child on

Censuses can be used for troubleshooting, to maintain momentum in your search, and to help locate that elusive ancestor who seems to have evaded any form of civil registration.

the census form, who was five. So perhaps they married in or around 1875/6. In which case, what had happened to William Waddell? He was alive in 1870 because there he was on Thomas's birth certificate. So he had either divorced Mary or died between 1870 and 1875. I went to the death indexes and started searching. Straight away I found the record of his death, in 1871, only a few months after Thomas was born. Then I searched the marriage indexes and, sure enough, a Mary Waddle had married a William Wilson, a coal miner like William Waddle, in 1874.

But all this, while grist to the mill, did not solve the case of the disappearing Thomas. I had a clue: I could search for him again under Waddle – though I had done that – or perhaps he changed his name to Wilson, the name of his new guardian. Yet both searches revealed nothing new. On a whim, I went to the marriage indexes and searched for a Maria Harrison, of which there were several between

1894 and 1900. I cross-referenced them to each and every variation of Waddell or Waddle, remembering that a misspelling of my name when I was at school had led to people calling me Widdle for several years. I checked Woddle, Weddle and Widdle. Bingo. In 1895 a Maria Harrison had married Thomas Weddle in Morpeth, Northumberland. I went to the 1901 census. There they were: Thomas Weddle, Maria Weddle and all the little Weddles. At some stage between 1901 and the birth of my grandfather in 1907, someone had decided to change our surname to Waddell. Thank God. I had found my great-grandfather at last, discovered when he had married and how he had lost his father as a baby and been adopted by another man when his mother remarried. In other words, the 1881 census had opened a whole new chapter of family history to explore, and offered a fascinating insight into how my name had developed.

< **In Lowestoft, Suffolk, on 27 December 1762, Thomas and Mary Day had their daughter baptized, naming her Christmas.** >

Inside New Register House in Edinburgh

SCOTLAND

The General Register Office at New Register House in Edinburgh holds the census returns for Scotland. Most are on microfilm, though the 1891 and 1901 censuses have been digitized and are available online. Excitingly, imaging of the census records for 1841, 1851, 1861 and 1871 is complete; surname indexes to these are currently being created and will go online at New Register House at some point during 2004.

IRELAND

Unfortunately, the census returns available at the National Archives of Ireland in Dublin are a bit piecemeal. Many were lost in a fire in 1922, while others – the 1861 and 1871 returns – were deliberately destroyed by the government. However, there are still several returns to search, and you might get lucky.

Did you know?

< **Before 1926 boys could marry at 14 and girls at 12, provided they had the consent of both their parents.** >

…the 1881 census had opened a whole new chapter of family history to explore.

AMANDA REDMAN

WHEN IT CAME to her family history, Amanda Redman, one of Britain's best-loved actresses, knew little but suspected much. Her father died in 1980 when Amanda was in her mid-teens, she has never felt able to ask her mother about their past. What she picked up was gossip and hearsay, one theory being that her mother's side of the family, the Herringtons, was in some way cursed – a belief vindicated for many family members when Amanda was scarred for life when she was only 15 months old after an accident involving a saucepan of boiling soup. There were rumours of illegitimacy, an abusive grandfather and mysterious uncles. The time came when Amanda wanted to know the truth.

To do so she had to speak to her mother, Joan, who lives in Brighton. It was the first time they had ever discussed the family's history, and it was an instructive conversation. She learnt that her mother suffered an extremely strict upbringing, her father, William (Amanda's grandfather) having been something of a tyrant who ruled the house with an iron fist. He served with the army in India, where Joan was born, and apparently was an excessive drinker. He left the army with a good conduct medal after 20 years of service.

opposite: Amanda with her daughter.

TOGETHER WITH her brother Anthony, Joan was able to fill in more of the family's story for Amanda, in particular the supposed curse that hung over the Herringtons. One of the most intriguing members of the family was Joan's half-brother, Cyril. It turned out that he was the illegitimate son of Joan's mother, Agnes. He had been born in either 1918 or 1919, before Agnes married William Herrington. Unsurprisingly, Cyril's relationship with William was fraught and, after a particularly grievous falling out, he went to live in Falmouth with his grandmother. The exact reason behind the row was never known. Then, in 1940, Cyril disappeared completely. Anthony spent 20 years searching for his lost brother, with no success, though his son, Trevor, has since taken up the quest. Intrigued, Amanda was determined to dig for more information.

It emerged that Trevor had found Cyril's death certificate, which revealed that his life had ended in Liverpool. Trevor also believed he had married and had a child. Amanda wanted to see if she could find this cousin she had never met. To do so she travelled to Falmouth in Cornwall, where she was able to find a friend of Cyril's, Desmond McCarthy. He said that Cyril had been bullied and rejected by his stepfather because of his illegitimacy. In the first half of the twentieth century illegitimacy was still a taboo, and given the almost Victorian values William had been raised with, it is quite clear he had no time for a child fathered by another man. During his teenage years in Falmouth, Cyril went through a rebellious phase: he stole a train, which resulted in his being sent to a reform school. Amanda also learnt that he had an affair with a local woman, who gave birth to his child, called Derek. Apparently the affair lasted on and off for 10 or so years, until the woman's husband issued her an ultimatum: choose him or Cyril. She chose her husband. Unfortunately, Amanda was to discover that the child of the affair, Derek, died a few years ago. She did get to meet Cyril's lover, though, who was able to tell her about him and their liaison. She subsequently found out that Cyril's child from his marriage was alive and well, and living in Liverpool. Amanda paid Karen Herrington a visit.

The reunion was an emotional one, proof that family history is not always about going further and further back into the past. It is possible to use your research to 'bounce back,' into the present to find living relatives you never knew you had. Of course, should you choose to locate living relatives, you must always be prepared that they might not react in the manner you hope or expect. It's not every day that people are contacted by someone claiming to be a member of their family, and their first reaction might be suspicion.

This was not a problem for Karen and Amanda; they were delighted to meet one another and fill in the gaps in their respective family histories. Karen was able to tell Amanda all about Cyril and William's troubled relationship. It turned out that Cyril had confronted William because he had broken Agnes's nose in a domestic argument. The resulting row led Cyril to leave home, and he never saw any members of his immediate family again. Amanda was fascinated and wanted to know more about her grandfather's character and his abusive nature. Now she was beginning to uncover all the dark secrets that had swirled around her childhood.

top: Amanda's great-grandfather, John Clair.
bottom: Amanda's great-grandmother, Angelina Youngman.

Joan, her mother, confirmed that William was a strict disciplinarian and that everyone was terrified of him, so much so that when he entered the house the atmosphere changed. Agnes had been a timid woman around her husband and, perhaps understandably, was unwilling to confront him about his bullying behaviour. Joan also confirmed that he would frequently beat the children. His drinking, a problem confirmed by his army records, compounded his abusive nature.

To understand her grandfather Amanda felt she needed to learn more about his upbringing. Why had he become an angry, remote and violent man? His father was a John Clair, who had married Angelina Youngman in 1884, at the height of Queen Victoria's reign. Through a surviving relative – William's niece – who had met John, Amanda was given a glimpse of his character and his family life. John was an incredibly strict father, a strict moralist and devout Christian who also had a difficult relationship with his children. Angelina was a different matter; her children adored her. Amanda found out that, despite becoming a middle-class Victorian housewife, her great-grandmother had also been born illegitimate. Patterns often run in families and similar fates frequently befall different generations – one of the intriguing aspects of family history.

Angelina's story was like something from *Oliver Twist*. Her father, it was rumoured, was a Dr Sweeting – her mother, Susan, had been his housekeeper. The pair had seemingly conducted an affair and it is thought that, when Susan became pregnant, Dr Sweeting decided a man of his standing could not lower himself to marry a domestic servant, so dispatched Susan to the workhouse to have her child. Somehow, despite

these inauspicious beginnings, she had met and married John Clair.

After investigating her grandfather's line, Amanda turned her attention to her grandmother, Agnes. How did she, a 'fallen woman', come to meet and marry William Herrington? To learn more Amanda took yet another trip to Falmouth, where she met her second cousin Val Laity, who remembers Agnes. Apparently, she was a withdrawn and reclusive character when William was alive, but when he died she cut her hair, painted her nails and again became the outgoing woman she had been before her marriage. According to Val, Agnes was of Irish descent, and it seems likely that her side of the family fled the potato famine that ravaged Ireland in the mid-nineteenth century and forced people to leave their homes in droves for England, the USA and Australia.

Val, an amateur genealogist herself, had completed some research and believes that Agnes was descended from the St Legers of Doneraile Court, an ancient castle in Cork. Descendants of Norman knights, the St Legers were sent to Ireland by Henry VIII to oversee the Dissolution of the Monasteries. One descendant of that family founded the St Leger, one of Britain's best-known horse races. This information provided Amanda with another path to follow – one that might reveal her previously unknown Irish genealogy.

The search for the truth about her family past was an exhausting and emotional one for Amanda. She had suspected there were some difficult truths lying dormant, and awakening them was not always an easy experience for her and her relatives. But exploring the difficulties, tragedies and secrets buried within family trees affords people a greater understanding of their family members, both living and dead. Amanda's journey into her past brought up some painful memories, but it brought her to a new understanding of herself and her family.

Now she was beginning to uncover all the dark secrets that had swirled around her childhood.

WHAT NEXT?

HOPEFULLY YOU WILL NOW BE WELL ON YOUR WAY TO ACHIEVING YOUR GOAL, WHETHER THIS BE LOCATING AN ELUSIVE ANCESTOR, TRACING YOUR FAMILY TREE OR DISCOVERING HOW YOUR FOREBEARS LIVED AND DIED. IT COULD BE THAT SIMPLY TRACING YOUR LINEAGE BACK TO THE MID-NINETEENTH CENTURY IS ENOUGH; THAT YOU HAVE DISCOVERED ALL THAT YOU WANTED TO DISCOVER. BUT WHAT IF YOU WANT TO DO MORE THAN SIMPLY SKETCH IN A ROUGH FAMILY TREE BACK TO AROUND 1837? THIS AND THE FOLLOWING CHAPTERS WILL HELP YOU TO FILL IN THE GAPS AND GIVE YOU A BETTER IDEA OF WHO YOU ARE AND HOW YOU CAME TO BE WHERE YOU ARE. BEAR IN MIND THAT FROM NOW ON THE SEARCH GETS MORE DIFFICULT AND YOU WILL REQUIRE PATIENCE, DEDICATION AND LUCK.

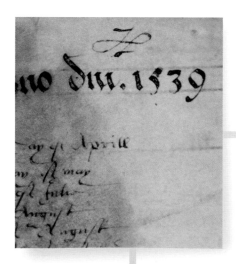

Name of Ship "Olympic". Date of Departure July 21st 1920. Where bound NEW YORK

Port of Departure SOUTHAMPTON. Steamship Line White Star.

NAMES AND DESCRIPTIONS OF BRITISH PASSENGERS EMBARKED AT THE PORT OF Southampton

Contract Ticket Number	Names of Passengers	Class	Port at which Passengers have contracted to land	Profession, Occupation or Calling	Age	Country of Last Permanent Residence	Country of Intended Future Permanent Residence
211612	Wilshinsky, Eva	2nd	NEW YORK	Wife	48		USA
	Ada				21		
	Viola				19		
4	Termeer, Henry				42		
	Irma			Wife	37		
8	Munro, Florence				43		
213131	Benthrol, Herbert			Barrister	18		
213238	Bowden, James			Miner	33		
	Alice			Wife	30		
4	Bailey, Thomas Hy.			Labourer	26		
8	Coad, James			Farmer	39		
9	Ferrell, William			Miner	36		
213321	Brooks, Leslie			Actor	16		
	Leach, Archibald				16		
	Harper, Patrick				22		
	Hart, Henry				18		

† By Permanent Residence is to be understood residence for a year or more.

GET BACK

IF YOU HAVE discovered ancestors who came to Britain from abroad, 'Moving Here' (page 120) will help you trace them and will also help you follow the journey of any ancestors who left Britain. If they served in the armed forces or fought in a war, 'War and Peace' (page 152) will point you in the right direction; and if you are interested in how your ancestors worked, where they lived and why – in short, how your family ended up where it is today – 'Path to the Present' (page 170) will help you in this quest.

But first we will deal with tracing ancestors who were born, married and died before 1837, beyond the era of civil registration.

The good news is that records of births, marriages and deaths were kept before 1837. The bad news is that not all of them have survived the ravages of time, some were poorly kept and, to the untrained eye, many are impossible to read. But parish registers compiled by the Church of England are an utterly essential source for anyone who wants to trace their ancestors back to the seventeenth or eighteenth century, and while the records themselves can be frustrating, the information they yield is often worth the effort.

Parish registers date from 1538, though many of the earliest records have not survived. Each parish kept a record of baptisms,

above: Emigration of Archibald Leach (Cary Grant) on the steamship Olympic.

The 1539 register of marriages, baptisms and burials at St Peter's, Dunwich, Suffolk. After this register was taken, Dunwich was destroyed by encroaching seas and was lost under the waves.

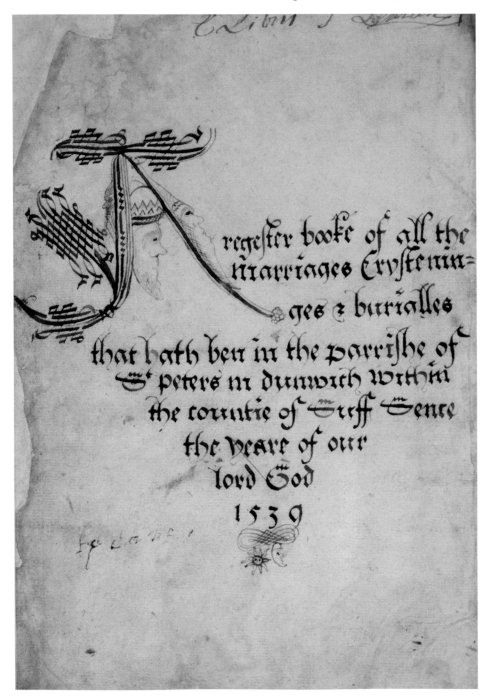

marriages and burials; sometimes in separate registers, sometimes in the same one. Great, you may think, let's start searching. The problem is that the information in these registers is often sparse, to say the least. It all depends on how conscientious the people who were charged with keeping the records actually were. If the vicar, rector, churchwarden or clerk who was responsible for the entries was a diligent, conscientious worker, the records you find may be of immense help in your search. If the same person was a shirker or a drunk, your search may be depressingly unproductive. Some lazy clerks might not have updated the register until the end of the year, and simply recorded the number of people who were baptized, married or buried, and no more. There were some 11,000 parishes in England and Wales, so the usefulness of the genealogical information you encounter will be a matter of pot luck.

Some registers carry detailed information; others don't. A baptism entry may only record the date of the christening, the child's name and the father's name, and not the mother's name. Before 1837 marriage entries did not give the names of the bride and groom's fathers; and burial entries usually gave only the names of the deceased, and perhaps their age. The records were often inaccurate, for the reasons already mentioned. Also bear in mind that, so far as the entries for baptism and burial are concerned, both events can take place several days or weeks after an actual birth or death (though one hopes that in the latter case it took place as quickly as possible). Do not despair, though. Entries get better and more detailed – and are also more likely to have survived – as the years passed, so working backwards from 1837 is easier to do at first and gets progressively harder the further you go back in time.

Did you know?

< **The census return for Ireland in 1881 showed an unprecedented number of deaf and dumb. Special inquiries were ordered – until it was discovered that the enumerators had included babies who could not speak or understand what was said to them.** >

NET NOTE

WWW.

If the Mormon Church brings to mind only weird marital practices and the Osmonds, think again. The kindly folk of the Church of Jesus Christ of Latter-day Saints in Salt Lake City, Utah, have compiled the International Genealogical Index, or IGI as it's known among the genealogical *cognoscenti.* **It includes millions of names entered from parish registers, though these relate only to christenings and marriages. It is by no means complete and is often inaccurate, but it can be extremely useful in pointing you in the right direction. It is a good place to start and can be accessed at www.familysearch.org.**

Locating the right register is another conundrum. Most of them are held at local record offices, though a few are still in the possession of parish churches. You will have to find the one that contains the details of your ancestors, which means you will need to know where they lived and in what parish. Maps showing the ancient parish system are usually also available at your local record office. It is worth consulting *The Phillimore Atlas and Index to Parish Registers,* by Cecil Humphrey-Smith, to find where registers are held. Your local library

may have a copy. Don't worry if you think you have the right register and there are no details about the people you are searching for. They may be in the records of a nearby parish. Once again, patience is essential.

If you live in the same area as your ancestors did, visits to your local record office will be easy. If you need to travel a long way, it is best to amass as much information as you can beforehand, to make your visit as fruitful as possible. Check on the International Genealogical Index (see above), and consult census returns going back to 1841 to ascertain exactly where your family was based. It may be that you are unable to travel to a local record office. If so, it is possible to get in touch with a local family history society, who may know of an expert who might be able search the records on your behalf, for a fee.

A number of registers have been transcribed. The venerable Society of Genealogists (SOG) is the resource for the largest collection. Go to their website www.sog.org.uk for more details, or pay them a visit (see appendix). They are near the Family Records Centre in London, and

> If you live in the same area as your ancestors did, visits to your local record office will be easy.

if you are not a member, it will cost you £3 an hour to use the library, £8 for a half-day and £12 for a full day. The SOG possesses Boyd's Marriage Index, which is said to include one in eight of all marriages that took place between 1538 and 1837. This is in the process of being put online at www.englishorigins.net where it can be searched (a fee will be charged).

THE NINE-MONTH YEAR

It is worth knowing that before 1751 Britain followed the Julian calendar: the Church year began on 25 March, Lady Day, and ended on 24 March. The Gregorian calendar was then introduced, with 1 January the first day of the year and 31 December the last. To catch up with these alterations there were only nine months in the year 1751: 25 March was the first day and 31 December the last. In 1752 the year started on 1 January and ended on 31 December. The old calendar was 11 days out by this time, so it was decreed that 14 September should follow 3 September.

READING **OLD** HANDWRITING

All the problems you may encounter with parish registers, such as sparse entries or difficulty finding the person you are searching for, pale into insignificance when it comes to reading registers from the sixteenth and seventeenth centuries. But do not abandon hope when you are faced with illegible squiggles or the odd bit of Latin. In the latter case, it is quite simple: common phrases you may come across are *baptizatus serat, nupti erat* and *sepultus erat,* which refer to baptism, marriage and burial respectively. If you are totally flummoxed, seek help. The same goes for illegible handwriting.

While the FRC has a deciphering service, local record offices don't, but the staff may be well versed in reading old documents or there may be a leaflet to help you out. You will find that the more old handwriting you read, the better you will get at deciphering it.

Old handwriting can be impossible to read and
play havoc with your eyes. Avoid myopia and ask
for help if you are struggling to decipher a
parish register as impenetrable as this.

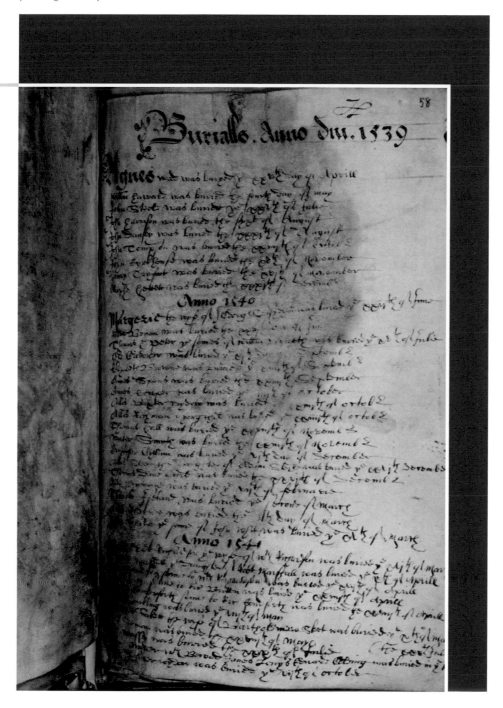

Nonconformist Registers

What do you do if your ancestors were not Anglicans? Don't panic is the answer. After all, as the 1851 census revealed, much of the country was Nonconformist: around 25 per cent of the population. So there is a good chance you may find that your ancestors were not members of the Church of England and were therefore not included in any parish registers. Nevertheless, it is not worth dismissing parish records if this is the case. Until the early part of the nineteenth century only Church of England baptisms, marriages and burials had legal status, and to keep within the law many Nonconformists held their baptisms, marriages and burials in Anglican churches. However, a number of Nonconformist groups did keep their own records and registers, many of which were submitted to the government in 1837 once civil registration began. These can be perused at the Public Record Office (PRO) in Kew, London, and the FRC.

Various Protestant groups were the most diligent in keeping records and registers: Quakers and Moravians, for example. Roman Catholicism is a different matter entirely. Few Catholics are of English descent – most are descendants of nineteenth-century Irish immigrants or European Catholics who came to Britain – and in the sixteenth, seventeenth and eighteenth centuries those who were were a persecuted minority. Catholicism was effectively outlawed, and fear of persecution prevented any meaningful registers being kept before the middle of the eighteenth century. In 1837, when Roman Catholic churches were asked to send in their registers, not many complied, and records are still often in the possession of the Church. The Society of Genealogists has some Catholic parish records, while details of fines and penalties imposed on people practising Catholicism (called Recusants) can be found at the PRO.

Did you know?

< **On the 1901 census, the late Queen Mother's middle name was spelt incorrectly: it was logged as 'Angelia' instead of 'Angela'.** >

The National Archives in Kew.

Until the early part of the
nineteenth century only
Church of England
baptisms, marriages and
burials had legal status.

TOMB IT MAY CONCERN

OF COURSE, SHOULD YOU WISH, YOU CAN GO HUNTING IN GRAVEYARDS FOR THE PLOTS OF YOUR ANCESTORS AND THE EPITAPHS ON THEIR TOMBSTONES.

If you are of a less morbid bent, the Society of Genealogists holds a national collection of monumental inscriptions. In case you are wondering how they have been collected – I did – local family history societies and other organizations have visited graveyards across Britain and noted down the inscriptions on tombstones and monuments: gravespotting. For the curious, it is well worth checking whether an ancestor's last communication with the world has been kept for posterity. Who knows, it could be as memorable as that of the English lawyer, Sir John Strange:

Here lies an
honest lawyer
Now that is Strange

DAVID BADDIEL

DAVID BADDIEL WAS BORN only 19 years after the end of the Second World War. Yet when he was growing up it seemed like ancient history. Therefore while his grandparents were still alive the interest he showed in their dramatic past was negligible, a fact he has come to regret. Also, the passing of time, and the birth of his daughter Dolly, prompted an increased curiosity about his ancestry and the struggles endured by his predecessors. Which is why he seized on this opportunity to delve into his ancestral history. David has just completed a novel, *The Secret Purposes*, which is based loosely on the story of his maternal grandparents, who fled the Holocaust, and focuses on themes of immigration and race – dominant themes in his genealogy.

David's mother Sarah was just five months old when her parents fled the Nazi regime in Germany in 1939 just before the outbreak of the Second World War. They arrived in Southampton with only the clothes they were wearing, a far cry from the comfortable life they had led in Germany prior to the rise of the Third Reich. David's maternal grandfather, Ernst Fabian, was the owner of a brickworks that employed more than a thousand people. He was a wealthy man and his wife, Otti, aided by a large domestic staff, spent her time hosting parties and working for charitable causes. They lived the life of a respected society couple. David visited the derelict site of Ernst's factory in Königsberg, now Kaliningrad, to learn more about the successful business his grandfather built, what he eventually lost and the family's desperate flight from Germany.

THE RISE OF THE NAZIS changed his grandparents' fortunes irrevocably. Humiliating directives stripped the couple of their wealth and their position in society. Ernst was forced to sell his business and the only way he and Otti could make money was by selling their possessions. Persecution of Jews grew and Ernst was in constant fear for his life. After Kristallnacht he spent a month in a penal camp and the Nazis gave him an ultimatum to leave or face an uncertain future. In August 1939 they fled Königsberg and travelled to Berlin, from where they caught a train to Bremerhaven and sailed to England. Sarah spent the journey asleep, safely hidden in the string luggage-rack in her parents' compartment.

At first Ernst and Otti were hoping to use Britain as a staging post on their way to Palestine. The British Home Office, which was attempting to restrict the number of Jews entering Palestine in order to defuse tensions there with the native Arabs, refused them onward transit. Instead, Ernst was classed as an 'enemy alien'. He had been in the German army in the First World War (ironically, David's paternal grandfather, Henry Baddiel, had fought for the Allies) and was awarded a 'B' classification – medium risk. This meant internment; he spent nearly a year at a camp on the Isle of Man. Only a few months after he had risked his life for his wife and daughter by bringing them to Britain, he was wrenched from them; he wouldn't see them for almost a year. As the father of a young daughter, the hurt and devastation this would have caused his grandparents are feelings David can imagine. His mother has more than 200 letters Ernst wrote from the camp, all of which describe the frustration of being separated from his family and give an insight into camp life.

When he emerged from internment Ernst was forced to begin from scratch, taking any type of work that was available to him: fruit-picker, hall porter, waiter, working in a factory. The experience of losing his business in Germany, and the humiliation of his internment, left Ernst a shadow of the entrepreneur he had once been, and he spent the rest of his career moving from job to job.

Despite their privations, Ernst and Otti were the lucky ones: they survived. Millions did not. Among these millions may have been Otti's brother, Arno, the black sheep of the family, whom Sarah Baddiel is convinced is her real father. She believes there is something unusual about her birth certificate but, despite David's research, no other evidence has come to light. Sarah thinks Arno might have visited his sister and her husband at the house in Königsberg and left her with them, knowing he was in danger and wanting to guarantee his daughter's safety. Ernst and Otti never knew what happened to Arno. As late as 1940 he was living in the Warsaw Ghetto, from

above left: 80th birthday party of Lesser Baerwald, David's great-great-grandfather.
above right: David.
middle: David's grandparents, Ernst and Otti Fabian.

where he wrote his final letters to them. David visited Warsaw, and from the research he carried out there, three possibilities have emerged about Arno's fate: he died of starvation or typhoid in the terrible conditions in the ghetto; he was deported to a concentration camp where he died or was killed; or, because his last known address was near the Jewish resistance bunker, he may have been killed playing a part in the Warsaw ghetto uprising of 1943. The truth will probably never be fully known.

The story of David's paternal ancestors is also fascinating. They left Russia in the 1890s, either for economic reasons, or because they were facing conscription into the Russian army where it would be impossible to practise Orthodox Judaism, or to escape persecution. In 1881, Jews had been made the scapegoats for the assassination of Alexander II. Pogroms were the order of the day: Jews were plundered and massacred, whole villages were destroyed and decimated.

Whatever the exact reason, David's ancestors felt the need to flee. One theory is that they left their home town on a hay cart, caught a ship to Riga in Latvia, which may have been bringing timber to the collieries of South Wales, and then sailed with it to Swansea. As Ashkenazi Jews from Eastern Europe they were looked down on by established Jewish communities who had immigrated into Britain earlier and viewed the new arrivals as 'rather foreign'. They would also have had to struggle against anti-Semitism in the local community.

The Jews in Swansea scratched out a tough life. David's great-grandfather, Barnett, worked as a 'schmatter' dealer, selling scraps of cloth and offcuts to textile factories. The business was passed on to his son, David's grandfather Henry, who found a wider circle of customers by buying a car in the 1920s. His profits benefited as a result and this relative wealth enabled the family to live in a respectable part of Swansea. It was David's father, Colin, who radically altered this branch of the Baddiels: he went to university, gained a Ph.D and became a chemist, working for Unilever.

Colin Baddiel is a secular Jew; he enters synagogues only for weddings or funerals. Henry, his father, was the first to break away, albeit partially, from his Orthodox roots when he married Sylvia Baumgart, the daughter of a successful East End photographer, and a secular Jew. Had Barnett Baddiel been alive, this union would not have pleased him – he was an Orthodox Jew so devout that he was instrumental in forming a new synagogue in Swansea because the existing one was seen as being too Anglicized. But while some Baddiels have broken with the Orthodox branch of their religion, others have adhered resolutely to the old traditions. Barnett's nephew – also named David Baddiel – was instrumental in the development of a community in Gateshead, Northumberland, that to this day is seen as the most Orthodox in Britain. He was a generous, pious man. Stories about him are legion: apparently he gave away so much of his money to charitable causes within the Jewish community that he bankrupted himself. He became treasurer of the Gateshead Yeshiva, seen as the Jewish Oxford or Cambridge. Descendants of David Baddiel are still well known within the Orthodox community. They know of David junior; know that he is a secular Jew, a comedian with a fondness for risqué humour and jokes about sex. They have never met.

As David's genealogy reveals, some Jews and their descendants, while adopting British nationality, have sought to preserve their way of life and Orthodox faith after arriving in the country, while others have cast this heritage aside and, though still retaining a sense of Jewishness, have become fully assimilated into British society.

Humiliating directives stripped the couple of their wealth and their position in society.

MOVING HERE

MANY OF US WILL DISCOVER IMMIGRANT BLOOD IN OUR FAMILY HISTORY. ROMANS, SAXONS, VIKINGS, NORMANS, JEWS, HUGUENOTS AND EASTERN EUROPEANS ALL SETTLED IN BRITAIN WELL BEFORE THE TWENTIETH CENTURY. IT HAS LONG BEEN A HAVEN FOR THOSE FLEEING PERSECUTION OR SIMPLY SEEKING A BETTER LIFE FOR THEIR FAMILY. REGARDLESS OF HYSTERICAL RECENT REPORTS ABOUT 'FLOODS' OF RAPACIOUS PEOPLE DESCENDING UPON AND DESPOILING OUR GREEN AND PLEASANT LAND, IMMIGRATION IS NOTHING NEW.

opposite: Planes, trains and automobiles: immigrants from the subcontinent arrive to start a new life in Britain.

By the end of the nineteenth century most towns and cities in Britain contained close-knit Italian communities.

BRITAIN HAS a proud tradition of accepting and integrating displaced peoples, and has, with a few exceptions, adopted a liberal, relaxed attitude towards them. So liberal, in fact, that unlike in other European countries, there were few restrictions on immigration until the twentieth century, and no compulsion on aliens to register their arrival. This makes tracking your relatives and their reason for coming to Britain a difficult, though by no means impossible, task.

You may have to travel way back in time to find them, however. After 1066 there was a steady flow of migrants to Britain, mainly from France. The flow quickened during the sixteenth century, for a variety of reasons – Protestants left the Low Countries to escape persecution, for example. More significant was the surge of Huguenot immigrants from France, where they were being hounded and massacred. Estimates suggest around 50,000 people crossed the Channel between 1540 and 1600. These foreigners were welcomed for the new skills and crafts they brought to England. Most of them settled in or around London, though some made their home elsewhere. When Louis XIV intensified the maltreatment of the Huguenots after 1680, even more sought sanctuary across the Channel. Because of this, many people will find that they have Huguenot ancestors, even Huguenot names that have been Anglicized over the centuries. So those of you who yawned during school lessons at the merest

WHAT'S IN A NAME?

IF YOU BEAR ANY OF THE FOLLOWING SURNAMES, IT IS LIKELY THAT AT SOME POINT IN YOUR FAMILY HISTORY – AND IT COULD BE HUNDREDS AND HUNDREDS OF YEARS AGO – YOUR ANCESTORS WERE IMMIGRANTS, OR EVEN INVADERS FROM A FOREIGN LAND.

FLEMING: a man of Flanders.

FRENCH: an early immigrant from France.

NORMAN: as in the lot led by William the Conqueror.

FRANCIS: means 'Frenchman'.

BEAUMONT: means 'lovely hill'.

GILES: An Old French miracle-working saint, probably brought by the Normans.

BRITTON: the Bretons who settled after the Conquest.

BURGESS: derived from the French word *bourgeois*.

BREMNER: settlers from Brabant.

NEVILLE: 'Neuville' – new place.

The Irish potato famine triggered a huge influx of immigrants into Britain.

mention of the revocation of the Edict of Nantes, or the siege of La Rochelle, could have been blissfully unaware that these were events that directly shaped who you are.

People kept on coming, mostly from mainland Europe. The French Revolution created an influx of French nobility avoiding the guillotine. By the end of the nineteenth century most major towns and cities possessed small communities of immigrants: Polish and Russian Jews who had fled the pogroms of the Russian Empire; Germans who had escaped the revolutions and uprisings of their mid-nineteenth century homeland (though many of them would be expelled during the First World War); and smaller, close-knit communities of Italians.

The biggest community by far was the Irish in Liverpool. The 1851 census reveals that 22 per cent of the city's population was born in Ireland. However, though they formed

Did you know?

< Poet William Wordsworth is an ancestor of *Austin Powers* star Mike Myers. >

close-knit communities, the Irish cannot be considered 'foreigners'; until 1921 the whole of Ireland was part of the United Kingdom. Many of these immigrants had arrived during the famine years of the 1840s, though for a long time before then they had migrated in considerable numbers.

The first half of the twentieth century was one of incremental regulation of immigration; the second half witnessed the era of mass

immigration. The outbreak of the Second World War and the horrors of the Holocaust prompted an influx of refugees from Europe. By the end of 1945 the Poles formed the largest group of Europeans in Britain. They were

> **By the end of 1945 the Poles formed the largest group of Europeans in Britain.**

actively sought in the period of economic rebuilding that followed six debilitating years of conflict, and formed, with other eastern Europeans, the European Volunteer Workers. These were joined in the late 1940s and 1950s by the first immigrants from the Caribbean, followed by those from India and Pakistan. All these people were welcomed – admittedly not by everyone – for their willingness to work, in particular to fill jobs the indigenous population was unwilling to do.

Throughout the past 500 years or more all immigrants to British shores have been touched by the hand of authority; some lightly, some oppressively. Yet this contact means that records were kept, of which many remain. It is simply a question of what they are, and where they can be found. The answer to the latter is, on the whole, the Public Record Office in Kew. This enormous complex – half pebble-dashed, beige carbuncle; half airy, modern glass box – houses all government records for the United Kingdom, going back to the Domesday Book and beyond. The records are said to occupy 170 kilometres (105 miles) of shelving. Most genealogists and family historians, however amateur they may be, end up at Kew, revelling

opposite: It's a great idea to take a digital camera along with you when you visit the PRO.

in the wide open spaces denied them at the FRC. The only thing you need to remember for your visit is this: buy a pencil. Pens are strictly forbidden.

But how do you find your immigrant ancestor? Let's assume you discovered he or she was an immigrant through information on a census return. It may be worth looking at later censuses because one of these might offer more than just the country where they were born. Perhaps a specific town might be mentioned. The census might also tell you whether they settled within a community – perhaps one, such as the Jewish community,

that was adept at keeping thorough records. They might have lived with and alongside their fellow countrymen. If so, why did they escape or leave their home country? For answers to these questions you will have to acquaint yourself with what was going on in the world at that time. You can track back and see whether any record was made of their arrival in Britain: were they registered by the authorities, or are they on the passenger list of the vessel that brought them? Did they become naturalized, that is, a British subject? It is almost certain that at some point they will have left a trace, however faint.

NET NOTE

WWW.

www.movinghere.org.uk is a welcome site that is well worth checking out. It boasts a database of digitized photographs, maps, objects and documents collected from 30 local and national archives, museums and libraries. There are histories of immigrants from the Caribbean, Ireland, southern Asia and the Jewish diaspora, and tips on tracing your immigrant roots. Best of all, there is a searchable archive of 150,000 items.

PASSENGER LISTS AND CERTIFICATES OF ARRIVAL

The first brush a new arrival to Britain might have had with authority would have been at the port where the ship that carried them docked. Since the end of the eighteenth century there has been intermittent regulation requiring immigrants either to register on arrival or to be registered by the master of the ship they travelled on. However, the piecemeal nature of the legislation means there is no guarantee that you will be able to find your ancestor. Time has also taken its toll: all that survives from records made between 1793 and 1815 is lists of aliens who arrived at British ports between August 1810 and May 1811. In fact, apart from certificates of arrival between 1836 and 1852, which give the person's name, nationality, profession, date of arrival and signature, and incomplete lists drawn up by the ships' masters between 1836 and 1869, there are few official documents until around 1878.

Passenger lists were kept from 1878, though only on ships arriving in Britain from outside Europe. If the ship's journey originated outside Europe and the Mediterranean Sea, those that boarded at a European port and disembarked in Britain would be included too. Unfortunately, if you do not have a reasonable idea of when the person you are searching for arrived, or don't know the name of the ship on which they travelled, your search could take as long as your ancestor's journey. The records described above can be searched at the PRO in Kew.

Note that because the Irish were regarded as British citizens, there are few records of their departure from Ireland.

Did you know?

< **The 1861 census has a return for a Coronation Street. A Mrs E. Sharples is listed as living there. Unfortunately her name was Ellen, not Ena.** >

Lists of incoming passengers, such as the one below, are invaluable in attempting to trace immigrant ancestors.

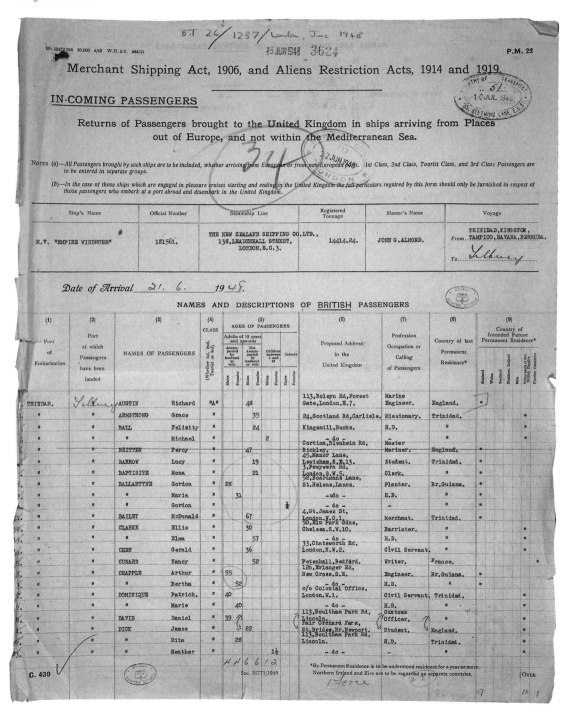

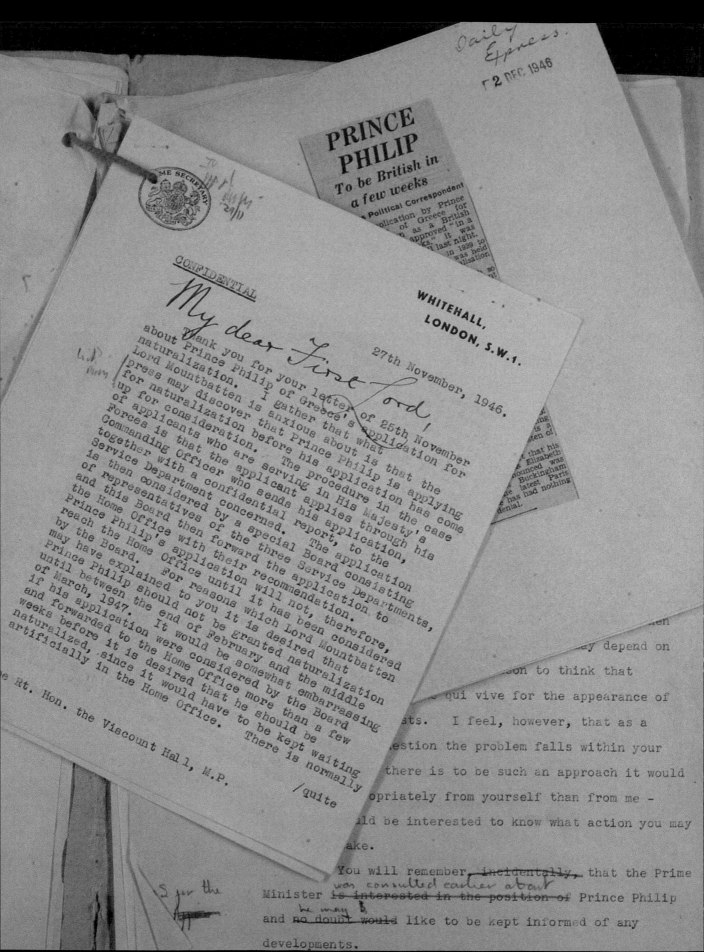

PRINCE
PHILIP
To be British in
a few weeks

By Political Correspondent

...pplication by Prince
...p of Greece for
...on as a British
...was approved "in a
...ks," it was
...d last night.
...in 1939 it
...was held
...alisation
...so

...that his
...Elizabeth
...nnounced was
... Buckingham
...e latest Paris
... has had nothing
...denial.

CONFIDENTIAL

WHITEHALL,
LONDON, S.W.1.

27th November, 1946.

My dear First Lord,

Thank you for your letter of 25th November
about Prince Philip of Greece's application for
naturalization. I gather that what
Lord Mountbatten is anxious about is that the
press may discover that Prince Philip is applying
for naturalization before his application has come
up for consideration. The procedure in the case
of applicants who are serving in His Majesty's
Forces is that the applicant applies through his
Commanding Officer who sends his application,
together with a confidential report, to the
Service Department concerned. The application
is then considered by a special Board consisting
of representatives of the three Service Departments,
and this Board then forward their recommendation.
The Home Office with their recommendation.
Prince Philip's application will not, therefore,
reach the Board until it has been considered
by the Home Office until it has been considered
by the Board. For reasons which Lord Mountbatten
may have explained to you it is desired that
Prince Philip should not be granted naturalization
until between the end of February and the middle
of March, 1947. It would be somewhat embarrassing
if his application were considered by the Board
and forwarded to the Home Office more than a few
weeks before it is desired that he should be
naturalized, since it would have to be kept waiting
artificially in the Home Office. There is normally

/quite

The Rt. Hon. the Viscount Hall, M.P.

...y depend on

...son to think that

... qui vive for the appearance of

...sts.   I feel, however, that as a

...stion the problem falls within your

... there is to be such an approach it would

...opriately from yourself than from me -

...ld be interested to know what action you may

...ake.

You will remember, incidentally, that the Prime
                    was consulted earlier about
Minister is interested in the position of Prince Philip
          he may b
and no doubt would like to be kept informed of any

developments.

opposite: Prince Philip, a Greek citizen, was naturalized, but as these documents show, the process was delicately handled.

NATURALIZATION AND DENIZATION

The choice facing someone wishing to start a new life in Britain was twofold: become naturalized, or undergo a process of denization, which sounds painful but in fact means becoming a British subject without the full rights of citizenship, such as inheriting land or holding public office. Naturalization was by far the less popular option because – other than when it was achieved by getting married – it cost money and the additional rights it granted were not seen as warranting the expense. Indeed, before 1844 a person could be naturalized only by an act of Parliament. Records of Denization and Naturalization can be found at the PRO, and there are indexes to these up to 1961, there and at the FRC.

ALIEN **CULTURES**

Before 1903 few restrictions were placed on immigrants and there was little inclination to do so. In that year a Royal Commission on Alien Immigration discovered that only passengers who arrived by ship were examined by customs officers, and that once immigrants were in Britain, they were not forced to register; the only information on how many there were in the country, where they lived and what they did was in the census returns. The 1901 census had revealed that out of a population of 41,458,721 there were 286,952 aliens residing in Britain. The Commission's report concluded that immigration put a strain on local communities, spread disease, increased crime and allowed anarchists and agitators into the country. In 1905 the Aliens Act was introduced, legislation which was tightened at the outbreak of the First World War when it became compulsory for all aliens over the age of 16 to register with the police. Some of these registers have survived and can be found in police archives or at local record offices. In 1920 the Home Office set up an Immigration Branch, which took control of and enforced immigration legislation.

Jews have been coming intermittently to Britain since the Middle Ages – and been expelled too, as they were in 1290. The majority of English Jews are of Ashkenazi origin (from the Hebrew word meaning 'German'). Thousands of Ashkenazi Jews entered the country to escape persecution throughout the nineteenth century, and many of them formed communities in the East End of London or in industrial cities such as Leeds.

There are papers and records on Jewish immigration at the PRO in Kew; the Jewish Genealogical Society of Great Britain has a wealth of information; and the Jewish Refugees Committee holds the personal files of up to 400,000 refugees, though access to them is restricted. Failing these options, if you know which Jewish community your ancestors lived in, there may be local records in a synagogue, or they may have been deposited at a local

records office. Be aware that records of Ashkenazi Jews can present a problem because they are often written in Hebrew or Yiddish. Specialist help may be needed.

There is one other problem when it comes to tracking Jewish ancestry: the way in which names became Anglicized as immigrants were assimilated into British society. The name Moss, for example, is often derived from the surname Moses.

SUE JOHNSTON

SUE JOHNSTON'S story revolves around the relationship between two men whose working lives reflected the increasing social mobility that followed the Industrial Revolution. The story of her great-grandfather, James Cowan, is an instructive one – an archetypal tale of rags to riches. He managed to pull himself up by the proverbial boot straps from the disease-ridden slums of Carlisle to become an independent man of means and even joined that bastion of the emerging middle class, the Freemasons. His son, Alfred (Sue's grandfather), rebelled against the plans his middle-class father had for him, and went to work on the same railways his father had used to haul himself out of poverty. While not creating anything as major as a family rift, it is clear that Alfred's independence corroded his relationship with his father.

James was born in Scotland in 1825 and later moved to Carlisle. Records seem to indicate that he started work on the railways around 1849, coinciding with the birth of the industry. The Industrial Revolution was changing the face of the country, and the railways were at the forefront. James spent 25 years working at Carlisle Citadel Station, one of the busiest stations in the country during the Victorian era. Seven independent railway companies were based there.

SUE TRACKED James's career path through railway records held by the National Archives. The records show that he started as a porter, rising to second head porter in 1856 and second assistant platform attendant in 1861. Family legend has it that he achieved the dizzy heights of station master. This, as Sue discovered, turned out to be untrue. He never made it to the top job, which could be the reason he resigned after a quarter of a century. The records show that he left seven months after the death of the previous station master, perhaps realizing that he would never step into his shoes.

Having spent many years living in The Lanes, a notorious, almost Dickensian, slum in Carlisle (now the site of a modern shopping centre), James had endured hard times. Sanitation was appalling and often families of 12 lived in one room. His first wife, Jane Harrison, died of tuberculosis, and three of their four children died in childhood. In 1866 James remarried, to Elizabeth Atkinson, and the couple had seven children. By this time his socio-economic circumstances had improved dramatically. His place in the middle classes was cemented, as the 1871 census shows, by the fact that he had moved into a townhouse and employed a domestic servant.

When James left the railways, he entered the hotel business, another booming industry. He enjoyed greater success in this field, and in the 1881 census he described himself as a hotel-keeper, employing seven domestic servants, at the Station Hotel, Belle Isle Place in Workington. On his youngest son Alfred's marriage certificate in 1909 he was described as a 'gentleman', further evidence of how well he had done for himself.

This success meant that James could afford the best for his children. Alfred, who was born in 1885, was educated privately by a governess. It is clear that James wanted him to get a respectable white-collar job, which he did, as a shipbroker's clerk, at the age of 15. But it obviously didn't suit him. Just as his father had chosen his own path in life, so did Alfred: this time, though, history repeated itself and he went to work on the railways – as a trainee

fireman and an engine cleaner. As the Station Hotel, his father's place of employment, stood right beside the railway track, Alfred probably grew up with the sound and smell of trains in his blood. Perhaps he watched them pass by each day and dreamt of becoming an engine driver.

Whatever the inspiration for his move, one can only imagine the family rows that accompanied his decision. James had spent his life working hard to escape the railways, a resolutely working-class industry, only for his son to choose it as a career. Alfred also married, probably unsuitably in his father's eyes, Margaret Lacey, the daughter of a plate layer. Perhaps the difficulties between father and son were generational: James was 60 when Alfred was born, so they were of entirely different eras. Alfred grew up at a time when the Labour Party was active and trade unions had gained some power. James, on the other hand, had had no support: he worked his way up alone.

After moving to Warrington, Alfred worked on the prestigious London to Carlisle line, eventually becoming an engine driver. Family myth had it

above: Alfred Cowan and Margaret Cowan née Lacey.

that he drove the famous Flying Scotsman, but Sue discovered this to be untrue. Alfred and Margaret had seven children, with more on the way, by the time of the General Strike of 1926. When the TUC called the workers out in support of the miners, who were in dispute with the pit owners about pay and working conditions, Alfred found himself on the front lines.

The government was determined to crush the strike, and put huge pressure on the union leaders to back down. After nine days, and despite the fact that more and more workers were rallying to the cause, the TUC gave in and ordered the strikers back to work.

Sue's quest ended where the story of the Cowans

She respects the way he went against his father's wishes to realize his dream.

began: in the border country of Johnstone, Dumfriesshire. It was here that her great-great-grandfather, James Cowan senior, and his family worked on the land as agricultural labourers, a punishing hand-to-mouth existence. Around the 1830s they migrated across the border to Burgh-by-Sands, a village just outside of Carlisle. From there James junior eventually moved to the city to look for work. This set in motion the Cowan family story, one of social mobility and advancement.

Sue has always felt a connection with her grandfather Alfred Cowan. She respects the way he went against his father's wishes to realize his dream of working on the railways, rather than remaining in a job he hated. She also admires the way he supported the General Strike yet still managed to support his large family. But her quest into his life revealed the awkward relationship he had with his elderly father, a man who had climbed a remarkable way up the social ladder, even for that time. The story of both men is a story of the railway boom and of social mobility, two phenomena that introduced new habits and attitudes to British life.

above: A Cowan family gathering.

MASS IMMIGRATION

The first Africans visited Britain as Roman legionaries around 2000 years ago, and people of African descent have lived in Britain for hundreds of years. In the eighteenth century several were celebrated personalities. The black community, made up primarily of seamen from the Empire, grew especially around the ports after the First World War. Following the outbreak of the Second World War, many colonists joined the armed forces and stayed in Britain once the war had ended.

After 1948 increasing numbers of people from the colonies arrived in Britain, starting with the settlers on the *Empire Windrush*. There were no barriers to colonial migration (and therefore no records other than passenger lists). This loophole was re-examined during the 1950s, when the authorities became aware that they did not know how many colonists were coming to Britain. Some industries and companies sought to recruit staff from the colonies – London Transport, for example, which brought many West Indians over to work on the Underground. In 1962, as a consequence of mounting public pressure and fear of civil unrest, the Commonwealth Immigrants Bill was passed. This introduced the era of managed immigration: colonists were allowed entry on the offer of a job. They were granted vouchers if they showed sufficient evidence of pending employment. Specimen applications are held at the PRO.

West Indian immigrants arriving in Southampton, 27 May 1956.

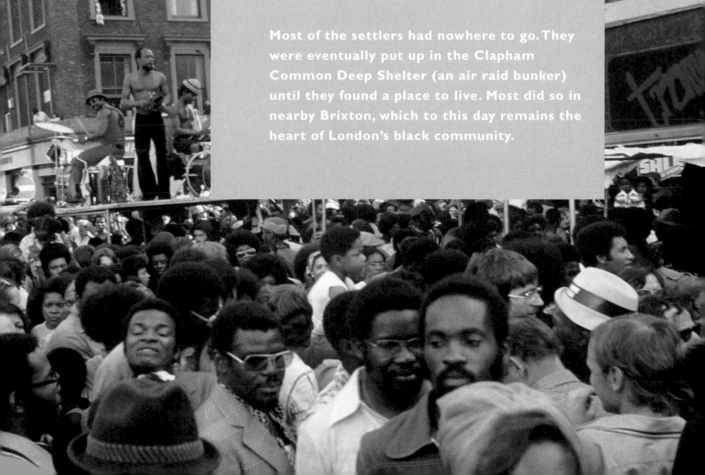

below: Notting Hill Carnival c.1970.

THE *EMPIRE* WINDRUSH

On 24 May 1948 the *Empire Windrush* left Jamaica with 300 passengers below deck, 192 above. Most of those travelling were women or ex-servicemen who did not know what fate awaited them in Britain. Some had jobs promised to them, mainly in the RAF. The majority, however, had no idea what they would do when they arrived. As the ship neared its destination, newspapers fomented public discontent at its arrival, and questions were asked in Parliament.

Most of the settlers had nowhere to go. They were eventually put up in the Clapham Common Deep Shelter (an air raid bunker) until they found a place to live. Most did so in nearby Brixton, which to this day remains the heart of London's black community.

MIGRATION
TO
AUSTRALIA
An assisted passage costs £10
APPLICATIONS FROM INTENDING
EMIGRANTS ARE NOW BEING
CONSIDERED IN THIS DISTRICT
ENQUIRE

... AND GETTING AWAY

It is estimated that during the course of the nineteenth century 10 million people left Britain never to return. The United States, Australia or one of the other colonies of the British Empire were the most common places people chose – or were forced to 'choose' – to start a new life. Before then, of course, many of the first settlers in America were of English stock. The best place to search for an ancestor who emigrated from Britain is in their country of destination, and some of the records held by the USA, for example, are better than those in the UK: passenger lists began in 1819 across the pond, compared to 1890 in Britain. You can look for your ancestor's name on lists for ships bound for destinations outside Europe from 1890 on. However, because there are so many lists, it is essential to have some idea of which ship your forebear sailed on, from which port and in which year, unless you want to spend months hunting them down.

> **Many of the first settlers in America were of English stock.**

Australia became a popular destination for British emigrants, but the government often discouraged non-whites from applying.

To Earn
More
Learn
More

OWN A HOME

VIC REEVES

VIC REEVES is one of Britain's best-loved comics. But that is all that Vic Reeves is: a comic character. The man behind the creation is Jim Moir, about whom very little is known. However, given the strange characters he has created, not least his often surreal alter ego, none of his fans would be overly surprised to discover that his family history was peopled with eccentrics and oddballs. Jim certainly hoped so. The idea of discovering an unknown scandal or a dark secret attracts many people to family history. Not all find one. Jim, however, did.

The person who fascinated him most was Simeon Leigh, his mother's father, who died in 1949. Simeon's father was a butler and Jim remembers a family photograph of him taken at Scarborough, Yorkshire, in which, despite never being wealthy, he was well-dressed and wearing spats. The only person with vivid memories of Simeon – a strong character – was Jim's mother, Audrey. She painted a picture of him as somewhat aloof and mentioned that he had been married before meeting her mother, Lilian, and that there were rumours that he was a bigamist and had been paid £400 to leave his first wife. The story was that he'd been given a first-class ticket to Canada, but had ended up in Huddersfield in Yorkshire.

SO WHAT WAS the real story? With the help of Nick Barratt, a researcher and expert in family history, Jim was able to discover that Simeon had been married twice: first to a Mary Jane Payne in 1900, and then to Lilian Crow, Jim's grandmother, in 1926. Marriage certificates could be found for both unions. The 1901 census revealed that Simeon and Mary had no children in early 1901; but a son Stanley Eustace Simeon was born in September that year. He was followed by another boy, Eric Trevers Edmund Leigh, in September 1903; and another, Clarence George Leigh, in March 1905. Twenty-one years after the birth of his third child Simeon married another woman; interestingly, on the certificate for his marriage to Lilian he declared himself a widower. However, extensive research at the Family Records Centre failed to provide a death certificate for either a Mary Jane Leigh or a Mary Jane Payne in the years before 1926. Was Simeon in fact still married to Mary Jane at the time of his second wedding? Had he been paid to leave the country, yet stayed in England and entered into a bigamous marriage with Lilian?

Bigamy was not infrequent in late-nineteenth and early-twentieth-century Britain. Divorce was a privilege of the wealthy and beyond the reach of most people. For many, it became possible only in 1937, when legal aid became available for divorce cases. Many married couples came to live apart, either by mutual consent or because one of the parties deserted the other. These separations could continue for many years, and sometimes one or both spouses wished to marry again. Such marriages were bigamous and a felony. Some people were naturally unwilling to risk a charge of bigamy and cohabited – 'living in sin' – or simply split up. But many others decided to risk a second ceremony and possible prosecution. Still others were deceived and did not know their marriages were bigamous.

Though it was against the law, there were two different types of bigamy – in the public eye, at least. There was 'acceptable' bigamy, where neither spouse had complaints about their husband or wife remarrying, and the local community knew of the situation and chose not to frown on it. On the other hand, there was 'unacceptable' bigamy, in which someone who was married deceived his or her new partner by pretending to be single. In Simeon Leigh's case the question was whether his bigamy had been acceptable or unacceptable. If it was the latter, he had been lucky to escape prosecution. Did his second wife know of the first? On his deathbed Audrey remembers him muttering the name 'Mary!' And how did this deception sit with the job he did before he died: that of church verger?

To find out, Jim went to Hull in Yorkshire, where Simeon and his family had lived. Simeon had worked there as a tailor, which probably explains his dapper look in the family photograph. Jim managed to track down the house they had once lived in, and also discovered that the daughter of Stanley, Simeon's eldest son from his first marriage, lived in Liverpool. He took his mother with him to meet his half-cousin Susan Reay, who showed them a picture of Mary Jane at Stanley's wedding. According to her, her grandmother was never divorced and never remarried, and was known until her death as Granny Leigh. We will never know the truth about the circumstances of Mary Jane and Simeon's separation, yet all the evidence points to the couple still being married at the time of Simeon's second marriage.

Simeon's father, Jim's great-grandfather, was no less colourful a character than his son. When Simeon was born his father, Simeon senior, was

top: Simeon junior surrounded by his second family in Scarborough, 1929.
bottom left: Jim's parents on their wedding day.
bottom right: Jim aged four.

living with his wife, Harriet, in Kensington, London, in a house inhabited by domestic servants, and working as a butler, probably for a wealthy local resident. In the 1880s the family headed off to Suffolk where – so Simeon junior's marriage certificate says – Simeon senior became an estate agent. In those days this meant running an estate, in Simeon's case for a wealthy industrialist, the delightfully named Sir William Gilstrap, rather than selling property.

This role was a step up for Simeon senior. Rather than heading up the domestic staff within the house, Fornham Park, he would have managed the estate, collected rents from tenants – which might not have made him too popular – and settled disputes among them. But as historian Pamela Horn pointed out to Jim, this was highly unlikely because the jobs of butler and estate agent were so distinctly different. Someone was not telling the truth. Could it be Simeon junior, practising deception once again?

Yes, was the answer. On Simeon senior's death certificate in 1909 his occupation was given as butler, and Harriet's described her as the widow of a butler. After feeling that he had been fooled by his grandfather's gilding of the lily, Jim decided to find out more about his great-grandfather's career. He was to discover a plot straight from *Upstairs Downstairs…*

The 1871 census listed Simeon senior as working as a butler for a Harriet Walker, at Money Hill House in Rickmansworth, Hertfordshire. Presumably this is where he met his future wife. Jim discovered that the couple's first child, Betsy, was born in Rickmansworth in 1874. A local vicar, the Reverend Alan Horsley, has written a history of Harriet Walker's family, the Athorpes, and told Jim

Divorce was a privilege of the wealthy and beyond the reach of most people.

that in today's terms Simeon's employer was extremely wealthy. She had originally lived at Dinnington Hall in Dinnington, Yorkshire, but after the death of her husband, Edward Walker, in 1869 she moved south to Rickmansworth.

It emerged that Jim's great-grandmother Harriet – one of the problems with his story is that the main protagonists share the same names – had been born in Dinnington. But this link between her and Harriet Walker was no coincidence. Her father, Edmund Leah, was gamekeeper at Dinnington Hall, and she was less than six years younger than her more illustrious namesake. Just to confuse things further, she married a man called Walker, who died. It is almost certain that she then served at Dinnington Hall; and when Harriet Walker née Athorpe moved to Rickmansworth, she took Harriet Walker née Leah with her as a member of her staff. There Jim's great-grandmother met and fell in love with her mistress's butler: Simeon senior.

Jim went to Dinnington Hall to try to find out what Edmund Leah's life might have been like as gamekeeper on the estate. The house and grounds may not be what they once were – the hall is now offices – but luckily estate records from the time still exist and are in the possession of Penelope Weston, a surviving member of the Athorpe family. Jim travelled to Yorkshire to meet Penelope and managed to find several logbooks that showed the amount of game Edmund was able to kill in one day. Ironically, while the amount of animals he killed warranted mention, there was no record of his death in 1852 – only the brief observation that a new gamekeeper had taken his place.

Jim's paternal grandfather, also called Jim Moir – or James Gatherer Moir to give him his full name – also led a very interesting life. Jim's favourite relative, he came from a long line of printers (all also called Jim) and our present-day Jim ascribes his love of words to this side of the family. His grandad was obviously a big influence on him and perhaps on his offbeat sense of humour – Jim recalls his grandfather telling him he still had a tin box from the First World War in which he kept the severed fingers of German soldiers!

WAR AND PEACE

MOST OF US HAVE AN ANCESTOR WHO FOUGHT IN A WAR, WHETHER HE WAS A ROUNDHEAD OR CAVALIER IN THE ENGLISH CIVIL WAR, ONE OF THE DUKE OF WELLINGTON'S 'SCUM OF THE EARTH' IN THE NAPOLEONIC WARS, AN INFANTRYMAN UP TO HIS EARS IN FLANDERS MUD DURING THE GREAT WAR, OR A ROYAL MARINE IN THE SECOND WORLD WAR. PERHAPS HE EVEN DIED WHILE SERVING. LUCKILY, GIVEN THE REGIMENTATION OF THE ARMED FORCES, MANY RECORDS SURVIVE AND THERE IS EVERY CHANCE THAT YOU WILL BE ABLE TO FIND DETAILS OF YOUR ANCESTOR IN THE FILES. YOU CAN UNEARTH INFORMATION ON HOW MUCH HE WAS PAID, THE PENSION HE RECEIVED IF HE WAS WOUNDED, ANY DISCIPLINARY OFFENCES HE COMMITTED DURING HIS SERVICE, AND ANY MEDALS AWARDED TO HIM IN WARTIME.

THE PRO HAS ALL military records listed in this chapter in its archives (unless we have stated otherwise) and it has published several easy-to-follow leaflets that are worth reading before you start your search. The FRC also possesses regimental registers recording the birth dates, marriages and deaths of all soldiers stationed in Britain between 1761 and 1924. The marriage records, it is worth noting, also include the details of the names, births and baptisms of children born to these marriages. If your ancestor served overseas, information about his birth, marriage and death can be located in the Army Register Book between 1881 and 1959, or similar books for the Royal Navy between 1837 and 1959, and the Royal Air Force between 1918, when it was formed, and 1959. Since 1959 the records of all three forces have been combined. Should you wish to obtain copies of any entries, each one will cost you the same as a standard birth, marriage or death certificate.

Many other records are available, and a brief guide to what they are and how to find them follows. For more detailed information see the books and resources listed in the appendix. Remember that at the PRO and FRC you should never shy away from asking the staff for help; they will be able to point you in the right direction should you have an idea of dates, regiments or the names of ships. For many people, the focus will be on discovering or confirming what happened to their ancestors during the world wars of the twentieth century. To this end, the chapter is divided into two sections. The first deals with finding details before 1914 and the second with searching for records pertaining to the First and Second World Wars.

BEFORE THE WORLD WARS

Before the Civil War of 1642–9 there was no regular army; earls, barons and kings raised their own militias and kept no formal records. Some records relating to this war – lists of regiments and their officers – can be found at the PRO. But better service records were kept from 1660 onwards, and most of these are also held at Kew, for both the army and navy, and for all ranks, including officers.

Knowing which regiment or corps your ancestor fought in if he was in the army, or which ship or ships he sailed on if he was in the navy, will save you lots of time, particularly if you are searching before the mid-nineteenth century because until then service records were commonly organized by unit.

It is equally important to know whether the person you are searching for was an officer or a common soldier or sailor. Records for ranks are different. You can, of course, wade through the Army List or Navy List, held on microfilm at the PRO. These give all officers, so if your ancestor's name does not appear, you can deduce from this that he was a soldier or a sailor – but it will be time-consuming. Knowing his economic background – put bluntly: was he wealthy or poor? – would help because, as a rule, officers were from the landed classes, and ordinary soldiers and sailors were working class. A few men from the ranks were made officers, but this was rare. Life as an ordinary soldier usually meant 21 years of harsh service, cut to six in the 1870s. As a consequence of the tough conditions of army and naval life, desertion was common. A sailor's period of service was between five and seven years; much of this was spent on half-pay on dry land, waiting for a posting to a ship.

< **Historians estimate that around 7.2 million British men fought in the First World War.** >

A SOLDIER'S **LIFE**

LIFE IN THE ARMY IN THE MID-NINETEENTH CENTURY WAS NOT A BREEZE. THE DAILY RATION CONSISTED OF 1LB (450G) OF BREAD FOR BREAKFAST AND 12OZ (340G) OF MEAT, BOILED, FOR MIDDAY DINNER, AND THIS FOOD HAD TO LAST ALL DAY.

Conditions in the barracks were squalid and overcrowded. As a result, many men deserted, while others sought solace in drink. Rare was the soldier who went though his entire service without some form of punishment for drunkenness. If you know which regiment your ancestor belonged to, it is well worth discovering whether there is a regimental museum. Even if the staff are unable to supply specific information about him, they will be able to furnish you with background information about life in the regiment at the time he served, and the campaigns he may have been involved with.

The Army

Officers

The PRO houses many collections, the best and most comprehensive being the Army List, on microfilm. It lists officers by name, and offers details on promotions, units served with and occasionally details of campaigns in which they were involved. A similar document, Hart's Army List, is also available on microfilm. The PRO holds details of correspondence concerning officers' commissions between 1793 and 1871, and there are also registers and correspondence about the payment of pensions to widows and their children.

Soldiers

Service records are the best place to start. Before 1883 these are indexed according to regiment (although there is a name index up until 1854 on microfilm). They indicate when and where a man served, where he enlisted and his age on enlistment, any disciplinary offences, promotions and reasons for discharge. Muster rolls, between 1732 and 1898, are the next-best resource, especially if you are seeking to track your ancestor's army career. They were compiled monthly and have details of a man's pay, offences committed

OFFICERS MENTIONED FOR SERVICE IN *Battle of Jutland on the 31 May 1916.*

NOTE RECEIVED 5.3.18.

PAPERS. *Despatch of 23 August, 1916.*   38.

NAME.	RANK AND SENIORITY	SHIP.	RECOMMENDED BY	NATURE OF SERVICES	GAZETTE DESPATCH OR REPORT G.D. or R.	AWARD IF ANY
John K. Cowan.	Engr. Lieut. Cdr. R.N.	H.M.S. Marvel.	C-in-C. Grand Fleet.	Kept his department in good order and kept the boiler water going in spite of evaporator being semi-disabled most of the time and out of action entirely for some period.	Gazette 31.5.16.	D.S.O.
Joseph A. Moon.	Fleet Surgn. R.N.	H.M.S. Benbow.	Ditto	was responsible for the excellent medical arrangements for dealing with the wounded in H.M.S. "Benbow", which were very efficient.	31.5.16	D.S.O.
Henry W. Finlayson, M.B.	Fleet Surgn. R.N.	H.M.S. Marlborough.	Ditto	A zealous and hardworking officer, who organised his department in an efficient manner for the action.	31.5.16	D.S.O.
Batram R. Bickford,	Staff Surgn. R.N.	H.M.S. Calliope.	Ditto	For great gallantry and devotion to duty in action. This officer, though severely wounded by a shell splinter, persisted in attending to the wounded, only yielding to a direct order from myself to place himself on the sick list.	31.5.16	D.S.O.
James McQ. Holmes, M.B.	Staff Surgn. R.N.	H.M.S. Castor.	Ditto	For the very efficient manner in which the wounded were attended to whilst under fire and subsequently.	31.5.16	D.S.O.

during that month and the location of the regiment. Medal rolls are well worth consulting if you have been told your ancestor was honoured for his service. The PRO has medal rolls for officers and other ranks going back to the Battle of Waterloo.

The Navy

Officers

The Navy List serves a similar function to the Army List: you can discover on which ships your ancestor served and any promotions he received. From 1840, you can consult service records. Again, these will tell you the ships he served on, any promotions he had and perhaps give some personal details. Other interesting documents include passing certificates, which were issued from 1789 onwards to prove the qualifications of officers, and were accompanied by baptism certificates.

Sailors

Before 1853 you will have to consult a few sources. If you know the ship, the first port of call for finding a sailor should be its muster rolls. Some of these rolls date back as far as the mid-seventeenth century and list everyone on board, carrying information about each sailor's age, pay and when he enlisted. For men who retired between 1802 and 1894 there are certificates of service, listing ships served on and dates of service. A final resource, and an interesting one, is the logbooks of individual ships, which may

GRAYBURN J.
GREEN G. A.
GREEN W. 1674
GREEN W. 22508
GREENWOOD G.
KELLY
KELLY
KENNE
KENT
KERSH
KETLEY
KIRBY
KIRMA
KITCHE
KITCHI
KNOX
LAING
LANE
LANGST
LANGT
LARVI

NET NOTE

If you are seeking details of a wartime casualty in either of the world wars, the Commonwealth War Graves Commission website at www.cwgc.org is a precious resource, well designed and easy to use. It boasts a searchable database of the 1.7 million men and women of the Commonwealth forces who died during the wars. A successful search will give you the rank, number, force, date of death and age at death of the person you are looking for. It will also provide details, if known, such as parents' names, place of birth, spouse's name and occasionally other useful information. Finally, but most intriguing of all, it tells you in which cemetery the person is buried and where it is, and gives brief directions for finding their grave. Should you wish to make a pilgrimage to pay your respects, links on the site offer information about cemetery visits.

> < **In his animated cartoon *An American Tail*, Steven Spielberg weaves a typical wide-eyed tale about a mouse named Fievel who arrives in the USA to embark on a new life. Spielberg's grandfather emigrated to the States from Russia; his name was Fievel. >**

mention sailors, though, more intriguingly, they will give details about voyages.

Service records were kept between 1853 and 1923 and include date of entry and discharge, ships served on, promotions, disciplinary offences and other personal details. Finally, as with the army, the PRO has medal rolls for those who distinguished themselves during their naval careers.

Be careful not to confuse the Royal Navy with the merchant navy – separate sets of records from the 1850s onwards survive for masters, mates and seamen who worked on commercial vessels, and who served on Royal Navy vessels on occasion or saw action during a war.

THE WORLD WARS

First World War

The service records for the First World War at the PRO are among the most popular and frequently searched. No wonder: approximately 6 million men fought in the Great War. There is every chance an ancestor of yours was among them. Perhaps you already know his fate; maybe he was one of the 723,000 who were killed, or the million plus who were wounded. Or was he one of the lucky ones? Maybe he was honoured. If you don't know, it is possible to find out.

The Army

There are three main sources for family historians, all available at the PRO. Service records are the best and most sought after. Unfortunately, it is estimated that a fire in 1940 destroyed about 60 per cent of the records of men who served between 1914 and the end of the 1920s. If you are one of the lucky ones whose ancestor's records survived, and have now been transferred to microfilm, you will be rewarded with the date of his enlistment, medical information and details of any offences, though the extent of the information varies. More records pertaining to officers survived, around 85 per cent, but they contain very little genealogical information.

The next-best source, particularly if you have drawn a blank with service records, is medal record cards. These are also on microfilm, and will tell you the medals your ancestor was awarded, the regiment he served with and where.

If you have found your ancestor and know the name of his regiment, it is well worth consulting war diaries. These are contemporaneous accounts of the action and daily life of units serving overseas. It is rare for individuals to be mentioned, and if a regiment saw battle, there is little other than a hasty scrawl, but diary entries can give you a wonderful feel for the life your ancestor lived.

The Royal Navy

There are separate service records for officers and sailors. Both give the usual information: date of birth, ship and an account of service. Records of the Royal Marines can be found here too. There are also medal rolls for all ranks. Bear in mind that the navy saw little action during the First World War.

< In the 1851 census Queen Victoria's occupation is listed as 'Queen'. However, despite her position as sovereign of Great Britain and its massive Empire, she was not even the most important in her house. The head of the household is listed as Prince Albert, her husband. By 1861 this was rectified and he is relegated to 'husband'. >

The Royal Air Force

Given that the RAF was formed only in 1918, out of the Royal Flying Corps (RFC) and Royal Naval Air Service (RNAS), few First World War records exist under the RAF banner. For details of the RFC look in army records; for the RNAS check naval ones. The RAF service records from 1918 give details of units served with, next of kin and other information – including rather catty comments by superiors on the person's flying ability. Medal roll cards provide information on medals awarded to RFC and RAF pilots, while naval records give details about those who served in the RNAS. Other sources that will add context to your search and offer nuggets of information on day-to-day operations are operational records and correspondence. All the above are available at the PRO.

Second World War

The armed forces were less unwieldy and more mobile by the outbreak of the Second World War than they were at the start of the First. Much of the battle was waged in the air by the RAF, and there was much more action

at sea. Be aware that service records are closed to the public for 75 years, though the Ministry of Defence will furnish next of kin and former servicemen with restricted details for a fee of £25. Also, no medal rolls are yet available, though awards for gallantry were listed in the *London Gazette,* whose indexes are searchable on microfilm at the PRO. If you are still keen to soak up as much as possible about the daily life and travails of your ancestors, it is worth consulting operational records. If someone was in the army, there are war diaries, while those who served in the air force often figure in operation record books, which give a fascinating glimpse into RAF life and provide details of every flight undertaken, as well as the crew involved. Fighter-plane fanatics have been known to get lost in them for hours and days, even weeks on end. There are less interesting sources if you are searching for someone who was in the navy: log books offer little genealogical information, though if you know the ship your ancestor served on, its captain's reports could make interesting reading.

LESLEY GARRETT

LESLEY GARRETT was born in Doncaster, in south Yorkshire, in 1955. The town, and its surrounding area, was predominantly working class – mining and the railways were the most prominent industries – and, on the face of it at least, her family was a typical, working-class, Yorkshire one. There was a difference, however, and it had an indelible influence on Lesley and her future: music. A talent for it appears to have run in her family for several generations, culminating in her status as one of the country's best-loved singers, who has done much to broaden the appeal of opera beyond its narrow, rather elite base. She has always cited her parents as her main, early musical influence, and recalls that she and her two sisters used to stand around the piano and sing in the evenings. But the musical gene isn't the only thing in her past.

Lesley's great great-grandfather was the greatest revelation. A butcher, farmer, and prominent member of Thorne Council, Charles Garrett had been kept secret from Lesley and her father – and not just because he was clearly set apart from their otherwise working-class family. In 1899 he killed his wife Mary, poisoning her with carbolic acid, which he administered instead of the medicine she was taking for her illness. Despite Charles being exonerated by the coroners' report, which stated a verdict of accidental death by his hand, the event caused a rift with his son Tom and daughter-in-law Mary, a keen temperance woman. Lesley speculates that Mary's temperate attitudes would not allow her to forgive an accident most easily explained as a tragic mistake under the influence of alcohol. Another side-effect of the rift was the decision by Mary to take her son away from the family butchers' business and into the railways – placing the family permanently in the industrial skilled working classes.

THE STORY of Lesley's biggest musical influence, her maternal grandfather, Colin Wall, is fascinating. One of eight children, he was born in 1897 with a chronically weak chest. At that time the only cure for his ailment was thought to be fresh air and as a child he was often forced to sleep outside when the weather was fine, for the good of his health. His father, William Wall, was a miner who had taught himself to play the concertina. When he realised that Colin's weak chest would prevent him doing manual work – virtually ruling him out of most jobs – William took sheet music out of the library and taught himself how to teach his son to play the piano. It worked. In December 1915, at an extraordinarily young age, Colin won a silver medal in the London School of Music exams. He went on to make a good living as a pianist with a small orchestra that accompanied silent movies shown in cinemas in the Sheffield area. On Sundays, when showing films was forbidden, he and the orchestra gave concerts, using sheet music borrowed from the local library.

When Colin was 22 he met and fell in love with Elizabeth Mellars, the daughter of a travelling showman. The problem was that she was only 15. She was chaperoned by a woman called Shipton, who was left dumbfounded when, after the young couple's lengthy courtship, they announced their engagement. Family legend has it that she believed she, and not her young charge, was courting Colin.

The end of the silent movie era also spelt the end of the orchestras that accompanied the films. Colin lost his trade almost overnight. This coincided with the Depression and work was scarce, particularly for a man with his condition. But he was determined to make his living as a musician and, through sheer persistence, he got a job playing the piano at the White Hart Hotel in Thorne, near Doncaster. It was a bit of a come-down. Colin had been used to playing to well-dressed, well-behaved audiences, and now he found himself playing in a boozy pub. Lesley says that in order to make the job more fulfilling he used to start work early and play his favourite sonatas and overtures to the empty bar before the

drinkers drifted in. As time passed, so did word of these impromptu concerts. Soon music-lovers across the area were coming to see this talented musician play. When the Second World War broke out Colin worked in the shipyards during the day. Wielding a blowtorch eventually caused his hands to double up with ganglions, ruining his career during the day but he continued to play at The White Hart in the evening. When Lesley was a child she would sit and listen to her grandfather playing Liszt and Rachmaninov for her – something she remembers with obvious affection.

Elizabeth, Lesley's grandmother, was also from a musical family. Her father, Frederick, was a travelling musician. He ventured across the north of England playing to workers in places such as Whitehaven and Maryport, in Cumberland. The former was a major English port at the time, at one stage second only to Bristol and London. Maryport eventually eclipsed Whitehaven, as it grew exponentially with the demand for exported coal.

Frederick Mellars could have played in both places when they were in their prime, to packed pubs and clubs. He also appears to have lied about his age so convincingly that he was conscripted during the First World War and allowed to entertain the troops on the piano. Once his itinerant days were over he settled in Rotherham in Yorkshire, where he sold pianos. These were no longer luxuries; they were common items in all but the poorest households, the source of entertainment in the evening and the focal point for the families – as Lesley's childhood shows.

Her father, Derek, was born in 1930. He worked as a baker, spent time in the RAF and was a

above: Lesley's grandfather Arthur with his accordion and the Clivettes.

signalman on the railways. It was while he was in signal boxes, isolated on the Yorkshire moors, that he started to educate himself. He would borrow a book from the library, recite it and tape his recitation, and then play the tapes over and over to himself until he had committed almost the whole book to memory. He was driven to better himself, unwilling to accept his lot. This caused unrest among other members of the family, who were proud of their working-class heritage; they were unnerved by his desire to escape. Derek blazed a bit of a trail: he was the first of that generation of Garretts to own his own house, cultivated a passion for natural history, played the saxophone and made his own wine, which went down very well with the relatives whenever the Garretts had a 'bit of a do'. He eventually became a headmaster.

Music was, unsurprisingly, as much a passion for the Garretts as it was for Lesley's maternal ancestors. Derek's father, Arthur, was a railway clerk by day but a musician by night. Before the Second World War he played in a band called the Melody Makers. During the war he renamed it Arthur Garrett and the Black-out Boys, and had considerable success in dance halls. And after the war he was in the Clivettes, named after Clive, the publican in the pub where they played. According to Derek, Lesley's grandfather was no great shakes as a musician, but made up for this with boundless enthusiasm. He was a multi-instrumentalist, and continued to play the circuit until he was well into his seventies.

Arthur Garrett married Kathleen Appleton, whose father, Frank, is fondly remembered by Lesley. She recalls sitting on her great-grandfather's knee as a small girl. He was a giant of a man. He was a miner before the outbreak of the First World War, during which he fought at the Somme, catching a bullet in his shoulder. When he returned to the pits a cave-in caused a prop to fall on his head, which sent him into a coma. He regained consciousness after two weeks and, although he made a complete physical recovery, his personality had changed. Once a hothead, he was now calm and gentle. He was always interested in Communism, and his catchphrase was 'Russia will redeem the world'. He was active in the 1926 General Strike setting up soup kitchens and agitating for workers' rights, which eventually caused him to be blacklisted in his local pit. He moved to Thorne Colliery, which was willing to turn a blind eye to blacklisted left-wing miners. Frank was also a member of the Royal Antediluvian Order of Buffaloes, a sort of working man's freemasonry. In her autobiography, Lesley evocatively recounts her memories of him: 'I would sit on his knee and he would give me a threepenny bit and talk to me about the trophies that he had won in tug-of-war contests. I used to love to watch him wash at the kitchen sink. Only a man who has spent a lifetime in the blackness of the pits really knows how to wash like that. Naked to the waist, with his vest, shirt and braces dangling, he would lather and scrub and rinse, carefully and deliberately, every inch of his massive body, ending always with his enormous, cavernous ears.'

She would sit and listen to her grandfather playing Liszt and Rachmaninov for her.

top: Taken over 100 years ago, this photo shows the 1901 Thorne Parish Councillors. Lesley's great great-grandfather Charles Garrett is bottom row, far left.

PATH TO THE PRESENT

WHAT HAPPENS IF YOUR GOAL IS TO FIND OUT ALL YOU CAN ABOUT THE TIMES AND CONDITIONS IN WHICH YOUR ANCESTORS LIVED, BUT THE INFORMATION YOU HAVE DISCOVERED SO FAR GIVES YOU ONLY A LIST OF NAMES AND DATES, FILLED OUT WITH A FEW SNIPPETS ABOUT OCCUPATIONS AND ADDRESSES FROM CENSUS RETURNS? HOW DO YOU GO ABOUT PUTTING FLESH ON THE BONES OF YOUR RESEARCH AND LEARNING AS MUCH AS POSSIBLE ABOUT THE LIFE OF YOUR FOREBEARS? THE GOOD NEWS IS THAT THERE ARE MANY SOURCES TO RESEARCH. BY USING THEM YOU CAN SEE HOW THE IMMENSE CHANGES THAT OCCURRED IN BRITISH SOCIETY DURING THE NINETEENTH CENTURY AFFECTED YOUR ANCESTORS.

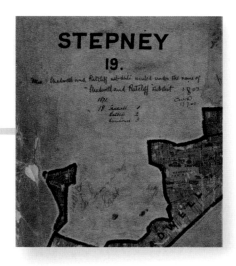

TRACING YOUR FAMILY'S PATH to the present can be done simply by looking at census returns and seeing where your ancestors were when the censuses were taken. But it might not tell you why the path took the turns it did. This chapter will equip you with the tools to discover more about how your forebears worked and lived.

DIRECTORIES

Trade and street directories are a rich source of genealogical and historical information. You can find them at county record offices or your local library, or if you are searching within a London borough, you can visit the Guildhall Library, which has directories that date back to the middle of the eighteenth century. The Society of Genealogists also possesses a large collection in its library.

Most areas published directories and it is possible to trace families and businesses through many years by using them. Following the fortunes of your ancestors over several generations is a distinct possibility. In many

working-class families the head of the household might have held a series of different jobs during his life; trade directories will help you to keep track of these. Likewise street directories. Between census returns, they can help you to pinpoint where your ancestors lived and exactly when they moved. Tracing them through directories can be less daunting than tracking them down on a census, and will save wading through acres of microfilm. With a specific address from a directory you can return to the relevant census and conduct a more targeted search. Trade directories also gave those with their own businesses a chance to provide more details of their services than they could give to census enumerators, while some might even have paid to advertise their wares.

Even better, searchable directories exist post-1901, the last census available to the public, which allows you to carry on your search into the twentieth century.

Be aware that directories may have been a year or two out of date when they were published, and that the amount of detail they contain varies between publications.

opposite: The 1900 Coventry telephone directory.

Directories published from the mid- to late nineteenth century generally feature more information than earlier ones.

Directories for specific trades, the professions in particular, also exist. The most famous is *Crockford's Clerical Directory*, published since 1858, which lists Church of England clergy; other well-known directories include the *Law List* and *Medical List*, which, as their names suggest, give details of barristers and doctors. Resources like these often have biographical information about each entrant.

Did you know?

< **Around 2000 surnames account for 80 per cent of the British population.** >

NET NOTE

WWW.

Though it is not exhaustive by any means, a visit to **www.historicaldirectories.org** can reap rich rewards. This project, run by the University of Leicester, aims to digitize selected trade and street directories and make them searchable for the general public. The site has excellent national coverage – nearly every county and major county town is represented – for the 1850s, 1890s and 1910–20. The last can be very useful for tracing ancestors found in the 1901 census. Searching is easy: simply type in a name or address and see what comes up.

Issue No.

MIGRATION: MOVING UP, MOVING DOWN

BRITAIN WAS TRANSFORMED DURING THE NINETEENTH CENTURY. IN 1801 THE POPULATION WAS 9.1 MILLION; BY 1911 IT STOOD AT MORE THAN 36 MILLION.

At the beginning of the century the population was predominantly rural; by the end it was urban. The flight from country to city spread across the land, and towns such as Manchester, Leeds, Birmingham, Bristol and Edinburgh grew exponentially as people left their rural birth places in search of work. London had 865,000 inhabitants in 1801; a hundred years later it boasted 4.5 million. Much of this can be explained by the Industrial Revolution, which, particularly in places such as Lancashire and Yorkshire, saw factories and mills making established cottage industries in rural areas obsolete. Britain became a varied, multifaceted place. New industries sprang up alongside traditional crafts, while other trades withered and died. Young people often left the bosom of their families and sought a trade in industrial areas. Social mobility was still restricted, though a new middle class was in the process of being born, but social migration was on the increase. Where once families had lived in the same area for centuries, people now moved in search of work, usually from villages and hamlets to the nearest urban centre.

It can be fascinating to trace the route your family took: the path that leads directly to you. I come from a family of coal miners in the northeast. From at least the mid-nineteenth century to the mid-twentieth century the male Waddells worked in the mines. This changed when my father won a scholarship to a grammar school; from there he went to university and moved away from the northeast, radically altering the family's path. Nebulous as such labels are, we would now be considered middle class. Who was the person, or what was the event, that changed the path of your family? Who knows – you may discover your family were well-to-do, perhaps members of the landed classes, then lost it all. Social mobility works both ways, down as well as up.

People who migrated from the country to the city to find employment in the mills of the Industrial Revolution were often forced to work in appalling conditions and live in grinding poverty.

opposite: There are no better sources than maps for tracing where your ancestors lived and seeing whether the house they occupied still exists.

LONDON METROPOLITAN ARCHIVES

IF YOU HAVE ANCESTORS WHO LIVED OR WORKED IN LONDON, YOU SHOULD PAY A VISIT TO THE LONDON METROPOLITAN AUTHORITY (LMA), THE LARGEST LOCAL AUTHORITY RECORD OFFICE IN THE UNITED KINGDOM.

Its archives are said to cover more than 52 kilometres (32 miles) – that must be one big basement – and they deal with a period of 900 years: council records; court records; hospital records; Poor Law records; parish registers; school registers; Nonconformist records; electoral registers; wills; maps; plans; prints and photographs. Its family history sources are on a database called London Generations, enabling you to search quickly. The LMA is an invaluable source.

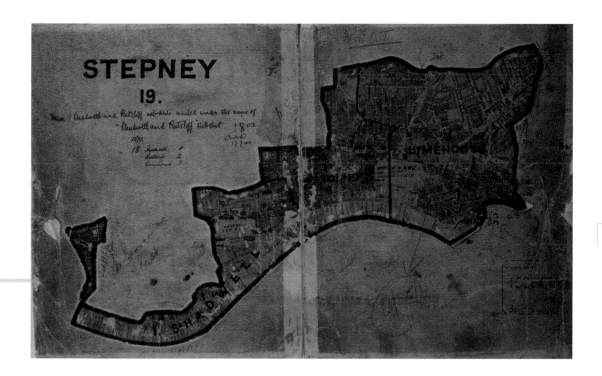

MAPS

The Public Record Office has in its possession 5 million maps. Of these, the amateur family historian need only be concerned with Ordnance Survey maps, first published in the early nineteenth century. So detailed are they that it is possible to find the house in which your family lived and track this address until the building was demolished. Of course, it may still be standing, in which case you will be able to make a pilgrimage to your ancestors' home. What better way to bring the past to life? Perhaps combine this with a trip to a local archive or record office. The PRO boasts a good collection of these maps, as do several other archives. Libraries and bookshops also sell reproduction maps.

Did you know?

< **Shakespeare died on his birthday, 23 April 1616, after having caught a fever at a 'merry party' thrown by Ben Jonson. In his will he left his wife Anne Hathaway his second-best bed. Who got the best one?** >

MILE END OLD TOWN

20.

24^B 1-2

1921971

1871

19

Mem. All that part of Mile End Old Town
Sub did. lying to the West of an imaginary
line running from the Northern boundary
of the District along the centre of Globe Rd.
across the Mile End Road & along the
centre of Whitehorse Lane to the Southern
boundary, transferred to
Mile End Old Town Western Sub did
1796

22 12 96

2. MILE

M R

I. — MILE END OLD TOWN WESTERN

24° 2F

These Boundaries do not app
to O1 Beaumont Square
Bethnal Green
2A
END OLD TOWN EAST

WHERE THERE'S
A WILL

Wills are an excellent and often overlooked way to bring your family history to life. Not only can they give you an insight into how members of your family were related, they can also provide a glimpse of your ancestor's personality – which, let's face it, hardly leaps from a marriage certificate or a census return. A minority of the population made wills – around one person in ten in 1901. But don't be suckered into thinking that only the wealthy did so: people of all classes left some last wish or request, even it was to bequeath a favoured flat cap or a best milking cow. There can be a list of the deceased's possessions – objects that will reveal how they lived – some of which could still be in your family, locked away in a dusty attic. Even more intriguing, wills can indicate family rows and grievances.

Often who is not included is more revealing than who is, or if someone was left a mere sixpence you can conclude that they were disliked, but had to be given something to prevent them objecting.

Finding wills made before 1858 is somewhat of a lottery – they are stored all over the place because there were several church courts that administered probate. Some are in the records of the Prerogative Court of Canterbury; microfilm copies of wills proved between 1383 and 1858 can be searched at both the PRO and the Family Records Centre (but bear in mind that before 1733 most wills were in Latin). The other main court that proved wills is the Prerogative Court of York. Its record of these is held at the Borthwick Institute of Historical Research

A minority of the
population made wills –
around one person in ten
in 1901.

in York, though indexes to wills from between 1389 and 1688 are held at the FRC and PRO. If neither of these sources has the will you want, a local county records office may have it.

After 1858 things get somewhat easier. In fact, because there are annual indexes for wills, it can be quicker to find out when your ancestor died from these indexes than from the quarterly indexes for death certificates. All wills proved in England and Wales are public records and can be consulted by everyone. They are held by the Principal Probate Registry on High Holborn, London, and can be searched Monday to Friday from 10 a.m. to 4.30 p.m. There are registers, or calendars as they are known, for each year, and they list all wills proved, the value of the estate and who the executors were. You will need to quote a

reference number should you wish to order a copy of a will, which will set you back £5. The FRC and PRO have calendars between 1858 and 1943 on microfiche.

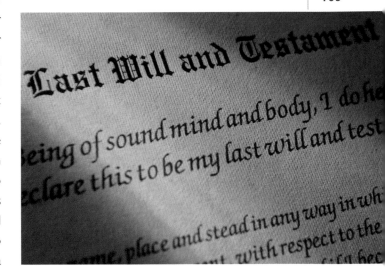

< The 1871 census has a return for an Albert Square in the East End of London. Most of the women are listed as 'fallen', the men as 'sailors', a sure sign that the houses in the square were brothels. There is no listing for a pub named the Queen Vic, however. >

In Scotland most wills have been deposited at the National Archives of Scotland. Indexes to Irish wills, even the many destroyed in the fire of 1922, can be searched at the National Archives of Ireland.

COPS AND ROBBERS

If there was a policeman in your family, there is a chance that the force that employed him holds records and will allow you to search them. The PRO holds service records for the London Metropolitan Police between 1829 and 1933, although these are not exhaustive.

Perhaps more interestingly, if one of your ancestors was a criminal – and the discovery of juicy titbits like this is the reason why many of us become interested in family history in the first place – it is possible to find a great deal of information about him or her. Some records are held at the PRO; others by local records offices. The PRO has those of the major courts: the Old Bailey, the assize courts. Local archives can throw up more interesting information because they hold the records of magistrates' courts and quarter sessions, which were concerned with more commonplace crimes, such as fornication. The quarter sessions dealt with a host of material: questioning applicants for poor relief, discovering the identity of the fathers of illegitimate children and administrative tasks, such as granting licences to publicans. Their records are not always easy to read, but sometimes the material they contain is gold dust.

In terms of other occupations, the PRO is home to records that can help to give you a picture of your ancestor's career. The railways were one of the biggest employers in the country, and when they were nationalized in 1948 the companies' records came under central control; these are now at the PRO. Each company kept its own records, so the extent of the information can differ. But you may be able to find staff registers, accident records and details of salaries and promotions. Of course, you will need to know the railway company your ancestor worked for and the type of work they did. The PRO also has records concerning merchant seamen and apprenticeships.

READ ALL ABOUT IT

Newspapers can be wonderful sources of information, particularly the kind you cannot find elsewhere. You may think your ancestors did not achieve anything newsworthy – but think again. Think laterally. Did someone die in an accident, or was his or her death the subject of an inquest? If so, the local newspaper might have reported it. The more horrific the details, the more likely something is to be in print. Since time immemorial newspapers have thrived on bad news with ghoulish delight, so any tragedies in your family may well have made it into the press.

For family historians, bad news is good news. Also, newspapers have always salivated over court proceedings, so the trials of any criminals in your family could well have been reported. Many newspapers carried – and some still do – announcements of births, deaths and marriages. People who made their mark on their community – or on the country as a whole when it comes to national newspapers – might be rewarded with an obituary. There exists no richer genealogical source, though, as is still the case, lilies were often gilded and reputations airbrushed when it came to recounting someone's life in print.

Unless you have a specific date, searching newspapers is difficult because of lack of indexes. But the national press can provide priceless information about what was going on in the world at the time your ancestors lived, while local newspapers can tell you what was happening in the community on the day someone was born, married or died. They can paint a picture of the life and times of your ancestors like few other sources.

Your library will possess back issues of local newspapers. The major collection of national and local newspapers, and periodicals, in the United Kingdom is the British Newspaper Library in northwest London. Indexes are few, though they do exist for *The Times* and the *Manchester Guardian*, as was – now renamed simply the *Guardian*.

APPENDIX

I hope what you have read here has given you the appetite to start searching for your ancestors and also equipped you with the basic skills to do so. Of course, the amount of information out there is limitless and this book only scratches the surface. If the bug has got you, there are family history groups you can join, magazines to subscribe to, hundreds and hundreds of websites to visit. There are two things family historians of all hues are not starved of: material, and people to offer a lending hand. This appendix gives contact details for the different archives and other organisations I have mentioned in the book. There is also a list of further reading for those hungry for more information.

Births, Marriages and Deaths

The Family Records Centre
1 Myddelton Street
London EC1R 1UW
Tel: 0870 243 7788
www.familyrecords.gov.uk/frc

General Register Office
(England and Wales)
P.O. Box 2
Southport
Merseyside PR8 2JD
Tel: 0870 243 7788
www.gro.gov.uk

General Register Office
(Northern Ireland)
Oxford House
49–55 Chichester Street
Belfast BT1 4HL
Tel: 028 9025 2000
www.groni.gov.uk/index.htm

General Register Office
(Scotland)
New Register House
3 West Register Street
Edinburgh EH1 3YT
Tel: 0131 314 4433
www.gro-scotland.gov.uk

General Register Office
Joyce House
8–11 Lombard Street East
Dublin 2
Tel: +353 1 635 4000
www.groireland.ie

Isle of Man General Register
Deemsters Walk
Bucks Road
Douglas
IOM
IM1 3AR
Tel: 01624 687039

Jersey Register
Office of the Superintendent
Registrar
10 Royal Square
St Helier
Jersey
JE2 4WA
Tel: 01534 502335

Guernsey Register
Registrar General
The Greffe
Royal Court House
St Peter Port
Guernsey
GY1 2PB
Tel: 01481 725277

National Archives

Public Record Office
(The National Archives)
Ruskin Avenue
Kew
Surrey TW9 4DU
Tel: 020 8876 3444
www.pro.gov.uk

National Archives of Scotland
HM General Register House
Edinburgh EH1 3YY
Tel: 0131 535 1334
www.nas.gov.uk

National Archives of Ireland
Bishop Street
Dublin 8
Tel: +3531 407 2300
www.nationalarchives.ie

Public Record Office of
Northern Ireland
66 Balmoral Avenue
Belfast BT9 6NY
Tel: 028 9025 5905
www.proni.gov.uk

Other Resources

Borthwick Institute of
Historical Research
University of York
Heslington
York YO10 5DD
Tel: 01904 321166
www.york.ac.uk/inst/bihr

British Newspaper Library
Colindale Avenue
London NW9 5HE
Tel: 020 7412 7353
www.bl.uk/collections/newspapers.html

Guildhall Library
Aldermanbury
London EC2P 2EJ
Tel: 020 7332 1862/1863
www.history.ac.uk/gh/gene.htm

London Metropolitan Archives
40 Northampton Road
London EC1R 0HB
Tel: 020 7332 3820
www.cityoflondon.gov.uk/leisure_
heritage/libraries_archives_museums
_galleries/lma

Principal Probate Registry
Probate Department
First Avenue House
42-49 High Holborn
London WC1V 6NP
Tel: 020 7947 6983
www.courtservice.gov.uk/
cms/3800.htm

Society of Genealogists
14 Charterhouse Buildings
Goswell Road
London EC1M 7BA
Tel: 020 7251 8799
www.sog.org.uk

FURTHER READING

There is a vast quantity of literature out there. These are some of the books that I have found most useful.

Bevan, Amanda, *Tracing Your Ancestors in the Public Record Office* (Public Record Office, 1999).

Hey, David, *The Oxford Guide to Family History* (Oxford University Press, 2002).

Kershaw, Roger and Pearsall, Mark, *Immigrants and Aliens: A Guide to Sources on UK Immigration and Citizenship* (Public Record Office, 2000).

Peacock, Caroline, *Good Web Guide to Genealogy* (The Good Web Guide Limited, 2003).

Rogers, Colin, *The Family Tree Detective: Tracing Your Ancestors in England and Wales* (Manchester University Press, 1997).

Titford, John, *Succeeding in Family History: Helpful Hints and Time-Saving Tips* (Countryside Books, 2001).

ACKNOWLEDGEMENTS

The author would like to thank Alex Graham, Victoria Watson, Ben Gale, Alex West, Victoria Greenly and the whole team at Wall to Wall, who gave their time willingly despite being phenomenally busy: Kate Carter, Kate Smith, Dan Hillman, Archie Baron, Hugo Macgregor, Lareine Shea, Lee McNulty, Anna Kirkwood, Katy Byrne and Mark Ball, thanks to you all. Nick Barratt's advice and expertise on all matters genealogical were also invaluable. Cheers Nick. Sally Potter and Sarah Emsley at BBC Worldwide were models of patience and understanding. Finally, many thanks to Julian Alexander and the wonderful team at LAW.

Wall to Wall Media Ltd would like to thank Jane Root, Maxine Watson and Tom Archer of the BBC.

BBC Books would like to thank the following for providing photographs and for permission to reproduce copyright material. While every effort has been made to trace and acknowledge all copyright holders, we would like to apologise for any errors or omissions.
Andrew Montgomery p 23, 35, 69, 87, 117, 137, 149; BBC Worldwide p 19; 16; 20 (both), 21 (both); The British Library p 106, 111; Cicely Lochhead p 18, 38, 57, 59, 61; Corbis/Bojan Brecelj p 11; Corbis/Catherine Karnow p 32; Corbis/Historical Picture Archive p 13; Corbis/Hulton-Deutsch Collection p 80, 82-83, 94-95, 144; Corbis/James L. Amos p 17; Corbis/Michael St Maur Sheil p 158-159; Corbis/Owen Franken p 162-63; Corbis/Quadrillion p 39; Corbis/Sean Sexton Collection p 125; Corbis/William Whitehurst p 183; Francesca Yorke p 51; Getty Images/Hulton Archive p 26, 27, 29, 67, 76-77, 114-15, 121, 134-35, 140-41, 142, 146-47, 164-65; John Frost Newspapers p 185; Justin Canning p 101; Mary Evans Picture Library p 74, 91, 122; Registrar General of Scotland p 99; Rex Features p 143, 167; Science and Society Picture Library p 176-77; The National Archives Image Library (with special thanks to Hugh Alexander) p 41, 42, 45, 78, 85, 105, 113, 126, 129, 131, 132, 156, 157, 179, 180-81; Mark Harrison/Radio Times p 2, back cover. All personal photographs appear courtesy of the celebrities and their families.

INDEX